D1447430

VIRTUE
AND
SELF-KNOWLEDGE

Jonathan A. Jacobs

PRENTICE HALL, Englewood Cliffs, New Jersey 07632

LIBRARY OF CONGRESS
Library of Congress Cataloging-in-Publication Data

Jacobs, Jonathan A.
    Virtue and self-knowledge / Jonathan A. Jacobs.
        p.   cm.
    Bibliography: p.
    Includes index.
    ISBN 0-13-942236-6
    1. Ethics.   2. Self-knowledge, Theory of.   I. Title.
BJ1031.J33 1989
170—dc19   88-5931
                                                    CIP

Cover design: 20/20 Services, Inc.
Manufacturing buyer: Margaret Rizzi/Peter Havens

 © 1989 by Prentice-Hall, Inc.
A Division of Simon & Schuster
Englewood Cliffs, New Jersey 07632

Printed in the United States of America

10 9 8 7 6 5 4 3 2 1

ISBN 0-13-942236-6

Prentice-Hall International (UK) Limited, *London*
Prentice-Hall of Australia Pty. Limited, *Sydney*
Prentice-Hall Canada Inc., *Toronto*
Prentice-Hall Hispanoamericana, S.A., *Mexico*
Prentice-Hall of India Private Limited, *New Delhi*
Prentice-Hall of Japan, Inc., *Tokyo*
Simon & Schuster Asia Pte. Ltd., *Singapore*
Editora Prentice-Hall do Brasil, Ltda., *Rio de Janeiro*

Contents

Preface

In this book I explain how an account of the nature of persons provides a grounding for objective ethical values and judgments. It is a teleological theory of persons and I speak unashamedly of such things as self-determination, the unity of a person's life-history, virtue, and the weakness of the will. I appreciate how difficult and controversial these topics are and also how unpopular they are among many philosophers. But I try to explain why they are the best resources to use in trying to understand moral phenomena and the character of moral reasoning.

I believe there really are characteristic human goods and that a right conception of our nature can help us acknowledge and explain what they are. They cannot simply be read off the concepts *human nature* or *person*. A complicated mixture of empirical, conceptual, and metaphysical issues must be dealt with. The conventions, habits, and practices that are involved in the moral dimensions of our lives constitute a kind of second nature. I believe it is essential to understand the primary nature they attach to and express.

I see moral philosophy as aimed in large part at articulating and explaining how what is good and what a good life is are bound up with what sorts of creatures we are. This is a very old view, but not out of date. I don't believe that the techniques and results of logical and linguistic analysis and the physical and social sciences alter the basic issues for moral philosophy. The latter must certainly be informed and aided by them. I hope that the present account shows how certain lines of thought that extend at least as far back as Aristotle are strengthened by their aid.

The guiding and motivating idea of this book is that there really is such a thing as practical wisdom; there is action guiding objective understanding that is not relativistic or merely conventional wisdom. What I try to explain in this account of our nature is what the object of that kind of understanding is.

AKNOWLEDGMENTS

Two of my undergraduate teachers at Wesleyan University, Eugene Golob and Louis Mink, who is sorely missed, deserve my thanks first of all. Richard Warner, James Ross, G. E. M. Anscombe, and P. T. Geach have guided, shoved, admonished, and inspired me over the last several years and I am fortunate that they continue to do so with exceptional generosity.

My friend John Zeis has helped me with vast amounts of encouragement and criticism and has taught me a great deal. I would also like to thank Sandy, Ian and Suzy Jeffers, Kate Wininger, Jim Anderson, and Keith Lodge.

Thelma Lyon and Bonnie Burdo, with the assistance of Louis Franco, typed several drafts of the manuscript, including the final one. They did so with patience and cheerfulness that still amazes me.

The Journal of Value Inquiry, International Philosophical Quarterly, and *Idealistic Studies* kindly granted me permission to use portions of my papers that they have published. The places in the text are indicated by footnotes.

We gratefully acknowledge use of the following material: A. Camus, S. Gilbert, trans., *The Stranger* (New York: Vintage Books, 1946) pp. 126, 127. Used by permission. A. Gide, R. Howard, trans., *The Immoralist* (New York: Vintage Books, 1970), pp. 111, 169, 171. Used by permission.

Introduction

Much of recent theorizing about ethics has been oriented toward the nature of practical reasoning, agency, the nature of character, and the virtues. This would surely be unremarkable except that for some generations of philosophy, at least Anglo-American, so-called meta-ethical concerns were focal. This involved a preoccupation with logical, linguistic, and epistemological matters and techniques. While this preoccupation yielded results that are not to be despised, it was a triumph of method over substance. In spite of the vast energy expended, it did too little work. It crafted valuable tools of analysis and clarification, but never wore them down on the hard core of substantive problems. Or worse, it either denied that there are any, or, as with Intuitionism, offered up quaint mysteries and the warm glow of subjective conviction that comes with initiation into them. This has motivated a return to the sorts of issues mentioned above, and a restoration of Aristotle and Kant to the center of the dialogue. Works by Anscombe, Geach, Foot, Donagan, MacIntyre, Williams, and others have restored a balance in the array of philosophical approaches to morality.

This treatment falls clearly on that side of the balance occupied by the authors just mentioned. My concern is with issues in moral psychology, deliberation, self-determination, and the way in which concerns about morality figure in a personal life history. This last item is crucial to my account. With Kant, I believe that a metaphysic of personhood is the mooring to which theorizing about ethics must be tied. The nature of persons informs the nature of morality. With Aristotle, I take it that persons, or rational agents, are properly characterized as having certain capacities for thought and action for which there are normative criteria of operation.

The main category, and the unifying idea of the present account, is the idea of a personal life history. I will show how the dimensions of certain basic issues in ethics are determined by the nature of a personal history.

There are different kinds of life histories. There are organic life histories. Sometimes we even speak of the life history of a philosophy department, civilization, or a banking system. These types of life histories are analogously related to each other through a common sense they all share. This shared sense is that a life history, in contrast to a mere series or collection of events or processes, involves some sort of continuity of development. The events or processes are unified through their relation to some end they are (successfully or unsuccessfully) directed toward. I believe that the notion of a life history is a *teleological* notion. The character of virtue and vice, the motivation to be moral, the spectrum of attitudes and responses persons have toward themselves and others are grounded in the distinctive qualities of the kind of life history persons have.

The distinctive character of a personal life history will be focal in this account. It will prove to be a rich character involving considerations about deliberation, rationality, and normative judgment. A person's teleology is full fledged, in that persons can choose which ends to pursue, reason about them, schedule their pursuit, and adopt attitudes toward their own activities and the activities of others. There will be special emphasis on the historical dimension of the exercise of persons' capacities—how they constitute a person's life not just formally, but as a temporally extended process and one the individual can think about and appraise. This issue is related to but distinct from the issue of personal *identity*. The formal and causal aspects of personal identity typically exercise us very little if at all. But we are concerned with our past and future and how they are connected to the present. I do not think personal identity is irrelevant or unimportant, but it is not at issue here. Rather I am concerned with the interpretive and explanatory perspectives we have that often figure heavily in deciding how to go on, what went wrong, what is really open to us, and why and how all this matters.

I contend that these interpretive and explanatory perspectives matter a great deal. I will argue that how a person thinks about his or her life history plays a constituting role in unifying it. This is important because we think of our lives in the category of unity, rather than identity. Unity *matters* to people in a way that identity does not. The latter is typically presupposed, while the former is something achieved. One of my main theses will be that being virtuous can make a decisive contribution to self-knowledge and the intelligibility and unity of one's life history. This claim covers both metaphysical and phenomenological aspects.

Much has been written recently about subjectivity, perspective, and the special perspectival location in the world of knowers and doers. We have had discussions of what it is like to be a bat or a brain in a vat. This book attempts to say something about what it is like to be moral and addresses subjective and objective dimensions of the issue. I should say at the outset that I am not at all sure that there are rational or any other sorts of considerations that can compel one to be moral. I do not mean to suggest that morality is not rationally grounded. There are objective moral considerations and reasons, and very good reasons to be moral. But there is no *argument* that will bring someone around to that side. Even if there is a correct theory about human or personal nature that grounds a theory of morality, it doesn't follow that anyone (even someone who understands it) acts in accord with that moral theory. The difficulty is not captured by the familiar "you can't derive ought from is" formulation. The problem is not is-ought, but ought-will.[1] I will try to show that one of the reasons to be moral is that it is enjoyable in a distinctive way. The context of persons is a moral context because we are purposive, self-directing agents. I will argue that being moral is the fullest expression of personal agency. It is the maximal exercise of the causality persons are capable of. Moreover, persons typically enjoy and find worthwhile the exercise of their agency. Its most complete operation, virtue, yields the richest and most stable type of enjoyment.

I remarked that to understand the nature of persons we must understand the nature of a personal life history. I suggested that the unity of a personal life history is constructed and self-imposed. It is achieved through an interpretive and explanatory account of oneself that the individual supplies to himself. Through this account, which I call a *personal narrative*, the individual achieves a perspective upon his past and present and an orientation toward the future.

These claims about how the unity of a personal life history is constituted will be connected with what I call the *Intelligibility Thesis,* that the more fully one's causality determines actions and dispositions, the more fully able the agent is to understand those actions and dispositions. Being moral can make a decisive contribution to having a coherent, lucid personal

---

[1] Aquinas, q. 58, Art 2 of *Summa Theologica*, states:

> For the appetitive part obeys the reason, not instantaneously, but with a certain power of opposition; and so the Philosopher says that *reason commands the appetitive part by a political rule,* whereby a man rules over subjects that are free, having a certain right of opposition. Hence Augustine on Ps. CXVIII that *sometimes the intellect marks the way, while desire lags, or follows not at all*; so much so, that sometimes the habits or passions of the appetitive part cause the use of reason to be impeded in some particular action.

These are expressions of just the sort of fact I am referring to here.

narrative. So while being moral is the maximal expression of one's causality as an agent, it also contributes to one's self-determination because if the virtuous agent is best able to achieve self-understanding, he or she is best able to go on successfully exercising capacities for self-determination. Opacity in one's historical self-understanding undermines self-determination. Through being moral one renders oneself free.

Despite the partial historicization of the nature of persons in this account, it obviously relies quite substantially on certain Kantian themes. I believe Kant is right that only rationally self-determining agents are moral beings and that through the virtuous exercise of agency one sustains and augments one's freedom. Kant's theorizing is much hampered by his obscure dualism of rational and empirical nature, in a way that, for example, Aristotle's ethical theorizing was not. This is largely due to the fact that Kant worked in a context marked by the conflict between mechanistic causality and rational agency. I will try to give an illuminating and explanatorily satisfactory account of the causality of rational agents that is not shaped by the categories that Kant inherited from Hume.

The focus of the analysis will not be on specific substantive issues of what is right and wrong. I am concerned with what is often called "moral psychology", as well as the phenomenology of morality. This will perforce involve a discussion of weakness of will and vice. So I will speak at length of virtue and vice, but will not be primarily concerned with delineating, defending, or illustrating specific virtues and vices. Rather, the book will emphasize the general character of virtue, weakness, and vice. I believe that formal characterizations of these are possible and have a good deal of explanatory import.

Any moral theory must meet at least two conditions. It must supply an account of the nature of moral value, and it must have something to say about motivation: how and why one would be moral. My account takes these to be intimately entwined, and the common thread is the concept of a personal life history. The nature of moral value is fundamentally related to what it is to be a person and, in connection with the Intelligibility Thesis, I will argue that the motive to be moral is as well.

This reattachment of the questions of value and motivation to the nature of persons is one of the more marked trends in current theorizing about ethics, bringing with it a salutary return to historical sources. I have indicated that some of the main lines of my account are Kantian, but not in any exegetical manner. Nor are duty or obligation going to get much play here. Kant's notorious excesses on those scores were (at least partly) a consequence of the dualism of rational and empirical nature I referred to before. Unfortunately, much of the criticism of Kant, especially the less subtle criticism, has been devoted to objections to the rigoristic breadth of his approach to the neglect of its depth. Kant had a clear vision of the fundamental connection between rationality, freedom, and moral value and motivation. He was not the first to reveal this connection. It has an ancient heritage. But the post-Humean problematic that Kant inherited lent a special urgency to his reformulation of it. Kant appreciated the urgency of restoring agency and reason in ethics. He is often the object of glib accusations of overdoing what could not be done at all, and his ethical theorizing is familiarly represented in disfiguring caricature. Its worst points are frequently emphasized as if any view that contained them could not contain any good ones.

One of its points, which I take to be among its better ones, is that virtue is self-imposed. One does not just find oneself being virtuous as one may just find oneself preferring the mountains to the shore. For Kant, the relation of the morality of an action to its cause was not contingent. I believe he was essentially right about this. Kant understood well the difference between being nice and being good, and that it takes a certain kind of strength to be the latter, and he often used the ideas of strength and fortitude in discussing the character of the will. Aristotle too placed significant weight on the role of rationally guided self-determination in virtue, though not in Kant's solemn and uncompromising manner. I will borrow from both Kant and Aristotle freely and often. My aim is not to make out a case for grouping them in some taxonomy of moral theories. Rather, I regard their contributions as the soundest fund of theoretical capital to be exploited, even if my own account departs from them in various ways.

The account in this book is, to a degree, a response to what I regard as a subversion of responsible agency. This is in large part a result of the combined corrosive effects of Utilitarianism, Relativism, and Determinism. These effects are not the product of a combined, systematic strategy. But there are several currents in thinking about the nature of persons, reason, and morality that over the last hundred or so years in particular have undone and putatively discredited a lot of much better thinking about those matters. This is not to say that we can simply go back. We can't. What I mean instead is that because of notorious problems about the nature of agency, the structure and scope of practical reason, and the character of normative judgment, we now have a tradition of ethical theorizing in which more and more of the distinctive character of morality and moral life was neutralized. The genuineness of agency, integrity, and responsibility were not so much questioned as rejected. The current atmosphere is much more congenial to claims and approaches that not only accommodate these but give them a central and fixed place. I sympathize with Kant's concern that persons should not be assimilated into a world in which scientific naturalism is regarded as omniscient. I do not endorse Kant's doctrine of the two standpoints. Instead, perhaps more hopefully, I believe we do not need to. He could not accept compatibilism and neither can I. His alternative was a theory of reason in which

the transcendental ideas serve, if not to instruct us positively, at least to destroy the impudent and restrictive assertions of materialism, of naturalism, and of fatalism, and thus to afford scope for the moral ideas beyond the field of speculation.[2]

I believe we can avoid these extreme measures of theorizing and still successfully account for responsibility, self-determination, and the moral dimension of our nature.

In this account I will develop ideas about the above-mentioned issues in the context of a view of the nature of a personal life history. I will not be elaborating a full theory of what a person is or of personal identity. I will instead attempt to explicate, illustrate, and tie together a number of observations about the nature of persons in an illuminating way.

A great deal of very valuable work in the logic, language, and phenomenology of morality has been done in recent years. This work is being connected with revived historical studies in a manner that does much to aid our understanding of practical reason, agency, character, and what persons are and why it matters. I will attempt to present a unifying treatment of these issues and developments. This account focuses on the nature of a personal life history because I take the concept of a person to be both descriptively and normatively central to an understanding of what morality is. The account is a theory of what might be called rational self-mastery; the theory common to philosophers as different as Aristotle and Kant that persons are self-determining beings who regulate their freedom by rational considerations. Or, at least they can, and this has a great deal to do with both morality and self-understanding. In Chapter 4, I consider some philosophical and literary sources from the nineteenth and twentieth centuries who have presented powerful critiques of this view. They object to the idea that self-determination has an intrinsic end grounded in our nature, and they object to the idea that rational self-mastery is a normatively privileged or even preferable condition. Authors such as Gide, Camus, Sartre, and others have shown how problematic and ambiguous freedom and self-knowledge really are. What much of this work shows is how the idea of the self must be broadened and deepened. There is an emphasis on subjectivity that is lacking in theorists such as Aristotle and Kant. Even though they did attend to issues such as conflicts of motives, they did not attend to problems such as self-interpretation as fully as we might need to. Their critics perhaps do this excessively. For Aristotle and Kant, the self is primarily a locus of rational activity, practical and theoretical. For more recent theorists, it is more a locus of interpretation and perspective. This difference is significant. I believe the truth resides in a conception that borrows from both. I do borrow from the authors mentioned, and in some respects I try to accommodate their criticisms and concerns. But in the end I see them as

---

[2]I. Kant, *Prolegomena to Any Future Metaphysics*, trans. P. Carus, Hackett Publishing Company, Indianapolis, IN, 1977, p. 103.

correcting the account and not undermining the conception of morality grounded in rational self-determination.

In the concluding chapter I address some issues raised by relativism. I believe that the general, logical contours of relativism are so twisted that the position is untenable. It also seems to me a way of deflating difficulties as a substitute for dealing with them. But it is important to discuss relativism, especially since I will be arguing that objectivity in ethics is possible. That a community can hold certain views of morality and personhood and engage in corresponding practices does not give those views and practices equal legitimacy with other groups' views and practices just by the fact of being held. Possession is no guarantee of a moral right to ownership. It is very easy and just as unhelpful to look on the variety of ethical and metaphysical standpoints and assess rational disagreement as delusory and rational criticism as merely ideological or contextual. There *are* genuine disagreements, and the actual and difficult work of issue formulation and resolution remains.

I will only discuss one sort of relativism, what I call the tradition-bound approach to relativism. By this I mean the view that moral conceptions and evaluations are essentially relativized to the conventions, institutions, and practices of specific traditions. I hope to show that while tradition is an important and pervasive feature of our lives, a kind of objectivity not restricted to this or that tradition is attainable. The sustainable claims for objectivity are grounded in the nature of a personal life history, and I will begin with that topic.

Chapter 1

Constructive Rationality and Self-Enjoyment

The structure of the life history of a person is constituted by the individual in a dual sense. In one sense it essentially involves the choices, reflections, judgments, and deliberations that the person engages in. These are actions in addition to all the things that we experience and have happen to us. In the second sense, a person engages in second-order reflection, interpretation, and evaluation of the above-mentioned. We construct conceptions of portions of our life histories and our life histories as unified wholes.

These unifying conceptions will be the main topic of the following chapters. In this first chapter I will make and explicate certain claims about agency or self-determination that express basic and distinctive facts about personal life histories.

What is a life history? Organisms and persons have them. We do sometimes speak of the life history of an automatic transmission or an idea or a corporation, but these are not literal usages of the expression. My claim is that those things that have life histories, whether organic or personal, have teleological constitutions. The events and states in their careers are not mere alterations. Rather, they contribute to (and may fail to contribute) the bringing about of an end which is developmental and not merely temporal. Organisms and persons have different sorts of ends and realize them in radically different ways. But the idea of changing toward a developmental end is, I believe, central to the notion of a life-history.

To avoid misunderstanding, we will have to begin by sorting out different types of teleology. An error as common as it is gross is to identify one type of teleology and either disfigure the others into it or eliminate them. Some things, like artifacts, have their teleologies conferred upon them. Whether it is something as simple as a screwdriver or as complex as a terrain-following guidance system in a cruise-missile is beside the point. The goal or end of the thing in the case of artifacts is conferred on it by an intentional agent. It does not inhere in the thing. Or if we want to say it does, it was put there by an intentional agent. Noticing this, many have quickly made a particular mistake about teleology. They reason that since artifacts' teleologies can be accounted for without any real respresentation of future states or action with reference to ends, perhaps all teleologies can be so explained. This is one of the considerations behind the current taste for functionalism. To eliminate obscurities involved with purposes, representation, and ends, so-called teleological systems are interpreted as *functional* systems, complex interrelations of causal operations capable of different physical realizations. So, differences between kinds of things, like artifacts, organisms, and persons are factored out of the analysis of how they work and replaced by the similarities of abstract structure of causal systems. This avoids both physicalist reduction and the bad old metaphysics of future states, and sometimes even consciousness. I believe that this approach, when extended in the wholesale way it often is, is mistaken. There are analogies between artifact, organic, and personal teleologies. But distilling them into abstract functional equivalents leaves out the real and explanatory fundamental differences.[1] Two points that are relevant here are: (i) that organic teleology involves not only functional organization and operation but also temporally-ordered, internally-regulated develop-ment. A good example of this is the equisitely complex economy of genetic activation and repression that controls differentiation and growth. Here we have processes whose matter is familiar to physics and chemistry, but which obey distinctively biological laws of development. (ii) I believe a very persuasive case can be made that organic functionality can only be realized in specific types of matter. As Aristotle pointed out: "Reflection confirms the observed fact; the actuality of any given thing can only be realized in what is already potentially that thing, i.e. in a matter of its own appropriate to it."[2]

A human cannot be made materially of cotton or glass and a geranium cannot be made of iron. Forms or functional systems can only be realized in certain types of matter. Aristotle's theory is neither reductionist

---

[1]See my "Teleology and Essence: An Account of the Nature of Organisms", in *Nature and System* (6) 1984, pp. 15–32, for a full account of what I take to be the teleological constitution of organisms. See also my "Teleology and Reduction in Biology," in *Biology and Philosophy*, 1, (1986), pp. 389–399.

[2]Aristotle, *De Anima*, 414a25. *The Basic Works of Aristotle*, R. McKeon (ed.) Random House, NY, 1941.

nor functionalist (at least in the sense being discussed here) and that is one of its virtues.

I will not say more here about organic teleologies except to remark that I regard organic life histories as being functionally organized and internally regulated careers that do involve nonmentalistic representations of future states. Similarly, I believe the teleology of a personal life history essentially involves representation, of past, present, and future. The chief difference between an organic career and a personal career is that for the former, the representation of the developmental end and what the end is, are fixed, given, according to the thing's kind. The entity's history involves end-oriented development determined by its representational system, but it has no choice over how and in what way the development is to proceed. A person does have the capacity to choose ends, deliberate about how and why and in what manner to pursue them, and to schedule and evaluate them. In neither the organic nor the personal context is teleology conferred from outside the individual. It is real and present in the entity, but in different ways. And that makes all the difference. If we do speak of representation at all in artifact teleologies, it is representation in yet a third sense. Artifact, organic, and personal teleologies are analogously related but not properly assimilated. It is just wrong to claim that if we can understand the teleology of an artifact along the lines of abstract causal structure, then we can so understand other teleologies. The idea of functional equivalence seems to me to require context derived from representational affinity; similarities in what states are represented and in what way. An array of physical objects is just not functionally equivalent to a cell or a portion of an organism's history if it does not exhibit representational affinity (which is not mere similarity of structural complexity). We ought also to remark on the difference between equivalence and substitutability. An artificial organ, for example, can be substituted for a real organ, but it is not equivalent to it.

The main point of these complaints about functionalism and the attendant interpretations of teleology is to preserve a real distinction between artifact, organic, and personal teleologies. The life history of a person is structured, unified, and conducted in a different way from even an organic history, though both are intrinsically teleological. The main point of difference is that a personal life history is constituted by the individual who has it, in the dual sense described in the opening paragraph of this chapter.

Persons are distinctive in that they are rational or have capacities for certain types of rational activity. It is the exercise of these capacities that determines the life history of a person. These are capacities for deliberation, choice, planning, and evaluation. Persons select ends, reason about them, and weigh, judge, and organize them into plans that they strive to carry out. One of the more central controversies concerning the nature of deliberation is whether it ranges over ends as well as means. We might say that this is a contrast between instrumental and constructive views of deliberations. In what follows I will make out a case for the constructive view.

I will argue that persons not only select and adopt ends but that there are some ends they identify with in a special way. I call these ends *motivational self-conceptions*. These are the primary or focal ends that an individual strives to realize and toward which he has certain evaluative attitudes. It is the pursuit of these ends that matters to a person in a special way.

The notion of ends, in the context of practical reason and action, is connected to the notion of desire. The simplest model of reasoning and action is that x desires y, believes z to be the most efficient method of achieving or getting y and so carries out the act accordingly. Some actions and action explanations are this simple. But only some. There is a lengthy catalogue of familiar and significant complexities. Desires occur in a variety of phenomenological modes. They may be simple or complex, sensational and episodic, or relatively long-term and stable. They may be welcome or unwelcome, regarded as base or noble. They may fit or fail to fit into an antecedent structure of values, interests, and goals. They may be irresistible or not. They may come in a flash or grow in strength and influence over a long period. And so on. The point of making these commonplace observations is that desire is essential to practical reasoning and action but not in just one or a simple way. Perhaps the best way to express the relation is to say that desire supplies an end, a that-toward-which reason and action may be directed.

Having a desire is a reason for acting, but we are not always moved to act in a certain way just because we have a particular desire. Often the end it would have us pursue is an object of criticism and reflection. This does not occur in a vacuum or with reference to the particular desire alone. We may find that to act in the way the desire would have us act is shameful, counterproductive, too risky, or too demanding. A complex and heterogeneous cluster of considerations can be brought to bear on the assessment of an end or the actions we contemplate as necessary to achieve it. Following through may involve means we find objectionable: hurting someone's feelings, unacceptable expense, or even a kind of courage we find lacking in ourselves. A person may desire to "stand up to someone" and really wish she or he would, but fail not just to execute but even to get started. At least sometimes a good deal of more or less complex consideration is involved before we are actually engaged by a desire, and how we are engaged by it can be modified by that consideration. Even those actions which follow easily and regularly upon a certain desire may involve a good deal of background explanation that a superficial account would miss. For example, someone may run to the library at the same time every week to check to see if a certain weekly periodical has come in. It is true, and for many explanatory purposes enough, to note that so-and-so loves to read that journal and rushes to check to see if it's there every Wednesday. But a fuller account of why he or she is such a faithful and eager reader may involve a good deal longer story; a story about his or her interest in its subject-matter, how it is presented, the person who is a regular reader of the journal next to it on the shelf and so on.

Desire is an essential component of rational action but figures in it across a broad range of modes. While it often initiates and determines action it is also often involved in deliberation and action in other ways. Making a choice, arriving at a decision about what to do, sometimes involves surveying alternatives, assessing one's abilities and opportunities, and locating the import of a possible action in a broader context of ends, interests, and attitudes. Persons, unlike non-persons, are capable of choosing from among their desires which ones will supply their actual ends. Of course, some desires compel and can move us "against our better judgment," as we say. Such a judgment need not be retrospective. Sometimes we knowingly do things we think we should not do there, then, or at all. But being moved in this way contrasts clearly with more or better reasoned action.

For persons, the question "what shall I do?" is connected with the question "how shall I live?" It is only for persons that this question arises and it arises inevitably, even if it does so in an inarticulate or implicit manner. It arises because persons experience openness with respect to ends and have the capacities to determine what ends to pursue. How persons live their lives is "up to" them in a way that is not open to other things. A person faces questions not only of the form "how shall I go about this?" but also of the form "shall I go about this?" and "what shall I go about?"

One's authority as a deliberator is not just instrumental. It is constructive in two ways, first, in the capacity to select from among desires, and criticize and evaluate them. It is this way that has been remarked upon so far. Second, it is constructive in the sense that deliberation can yield or produce an end or a desire to follow a certain course which was not antecedently desired. This is the more controversial thesis, though I believe a good case can be made out for it.

The influence of a basically Humean conception of the causation of action has sustained the vigor of the instrumental conception of practical reason and deliberation.[3] This conception involves a thesis about the scope of deliberation and a thesis about the character of the causality of action.

---

[3]Hume does say that "Reason and Judgment may, indeed, be the mediate cause of an action, by prompting, or by directing a passion:" (p. 462, *Treatise*, Selby-Bigge ed.), and that, "The moment we perceive the falsehood of any supposition, or the insufficiency of any means our passions yield to our reason without any opposition" (ibid, p. 496). But I would still insist that, for Hume, reason does not have the constructive role I am attributing to it. On page 425 he argues that reason cannot oppose a passion and that, "Reason is, and ought only to be the slave of the passions and can never pretend to any other office than to serve and obey them."

The first thesis is that all deliberation is motivated and directed by antecedent desire. The end is prior to the exercise of capacities to think about and pursue ends. The second thesis is that the "mechanics" of the causality of action are comparable to any other sort of causal mechanics. Both theses, if taken in this simple form and to have complete generality, are false. My main concern is with the former and the results of discussing it should indicate the reasons for rejecting the second.

Sometimes the application of the critical and reflective capacities mentioned so far results in the revision or rejection of an end. It is not merely whether to pursue it or in what way that is altered, sometimes the desire itself is modified. When one desires, say, to travel to a certain place, and "looks into it," what it is like, what it costs, what the experiences of others have been and so on, not just the decision but also the desire may be influenced. The character of the desire may be changed in any number of ways. Furthermore, the deliberations may yield a different desire. Consideration of one's criteria of an enjoyable, worthwhile trip and other relevant factors may result in an intermediate conclusion in one's deliberations, which is not an action but a desire; a desire to go elsewhere or spend one's time and money otherwise. The result here is not recognition of an antecedent but unacknowledged desire but construction of an end. Wiggins expresses a view similar to this. He states:

> In the nontechnical case I shall characteristically have an extremely vague description of something I want—a good life, a satisfying profession, an interesting holiday, an amusing evening—and the problem is not to see what will be causally efficacious in bringing this about but to see what *qualifies* an adequate and practically realizable specification of what would satisfy this want. Deliberation is still *zetesis*, a search, but it is not primarily a search for means. It is a search for the *best specification*. Till the specification is available there is no room for means.[4]

We often begin with a broad and adjustable conception of an end and the initial thrust of the deliberative process is to articulate and define it. Many of the actions for which deliberation is primarily instrumental require very little thought at all. Many of the things we want to do we just know how to go about doing, and the action is relatively spontaneous or habitual. It is where determination of the end itself and its position in our plans and outlook are undecided that deliberative abilities are employed in a more extensive manner. It is through employment of these abilities that we may come to a decision about what sort of career to pursue, what evening courses to take, or how to spend our inheritance. These sorts of

[4]D. Wiggins, "Deliberation and Practical Reason," printed in *Essays on Aristotle's Ethics*, ed. A. Rorty, University of California Press, Berkeley, CA, 1980. See also Chapter 5 of T. Nagel, *The Possibility of Altruism*, Princeton University Press, Princeton, NJ, 1970, and T. Irwin, "Aristotle on Reason, Desire and Virtue", *Journal of Philosophy*, November 1975, pp. 567–578.

decisions surely may be motivated by more or less powerful antecedent desires. But sometimes reflection or investigation yields considerations that we regard as reasons for modifying our desires. We might say, "I've changed my mind about the trip. Now I want to go to this other place for the following reason." And then we go on and account for our new desire, or new determination to act in a certain way, in terms of reasons. In the passage quoted from Wiggins he speaks of specifying more fully what is already wanted. Specification and construction of an end may involve desires which may be vague or even consequent upon one's deliberation.

With Aristotle, I believe that "Intellect itself, however, moves nothing, but only intellect which aims at an end and is practical; . . . Hence choice is either desiderative reason or ratiocinative desire, and such an origin of action is a man."[5]

I quote this passage to mark the difference between the view here and both the Humean and Kantian views. The Humean view accords too little efficacy to reason, the Kantian too much. The "mixed" view of Aristotelian heritage acknowledges the motivational requirement of appetition, but also the constructive efficacy of reason. If the agency of practical reason were limited to instrumental tasks, then competence or excellence in its operation would be mainly a matter of application of learned rules or of skill. But the resources of practical reason are more extensive than that. The Humean picture leaves out too much of the evaluative and critical component of practical reason. The Kantian picture leaves the issue of the motivational force of practical reason, at least as it operates in morality, deeply problematic and obscure. Both overformalize by detaching the form of the practical employment of reason from the matter it works on. It is easy to be unfair to Hume and portray his account in an overly simple and mechanistic manner. There is room in his theory for revision, comparison, and appraisal of desires. But he is quite plain that the causality of action is the same in kind as natural, "mechanical" causality. And he is also quite plain about the motivational impotence of reason. Neither of these matters is as plain as he makes them out to be. A more complex account of reasoning about ends and means is needed.

Not only do desires and ends come to a person or get formulated in different sorts of ways. Persons stand in different *relations* to them. It is plain that we align our ends on a value schedule. But the schedule exhibits more complexity than just differences in degree of importance. Persons *identify* with some ends and thus have them in a different way than others with which they do not identify. The ends with which one identifies are *motivational self-conceptions*. They are primary ends in the sense that they express not just what a person wants most to do but what she or he wants to *be*. They are those ends to which one commits one's agency in a special way

[5]*Nicomachean Ethics*, 1139a 34–1139b5.

in constituting his or her life history. This notion of motivational self-conceptions bears affinities to the notion of character employed by Williams in "Persons, Character and Morality."[6] His view is that "an individual person has a set of desires, concerns, or as I shall often call them, projects, which help constitute a *character*." A person has a character "in the sense of having projects and categorical desires with which that person is identified." A person can identify with certain ends in the respect that he regards his pursuing them in certain ways as crucial to his life's being structured and oriented in a certain way. Through his motivational self-conceptions he is concerned not only about doing such and such but that his doing so will contribute to his being a certain type of person. A person is capable of conceptualizing his life history as being directed toward certain ends for particular reasons through his own authority. Much of what persons do is not just intentional in the sense of knowingly bringing about what they desire, but involves contributing to the realization of self-conceptions.

Of course we might want to explain someone's coming to have a motivational self-conception with reference to their experiences and personal history in general. Reasons such as "he wants to fill his father's shoes", "she needs to feel that she is free of being controlled by him", "she's always had an idealistic bent" and so on may figure in the causal-explanatory account of why one has certain motivational self-conceptions. What one identifies with and commits to depends partially on how he or she sees the past, relations with others, future prospects and so on. These matters of self-interpretation and self-knowledge will be taken up in the next chapter.

It is not the genesis of an end that determines that it is a motivational self-conception. It is the attitude the agent adopts toward it. The ends may come to him as many other desires do, without deliberative rationality contributing to their construction. But their selection and the decision to hold fast to them is a function of deliberative rationality, even if its operation is minimal. Motivational self-conceptions are not given, they are "taken up." They needn't be especially noble or ambitious or even interesting. The expression is not intended to connote any high-mindedness. If it did it would falsify the phenomena. While we might think of "mastering Shakespeare's tragedies" or "becoming the Bronx district attorney" or "curing cancer" as examples of motivational self-conceptions, they may surely be a good deal less complex or demanding than that.

Suppose, for example, I decide to take up an exercise and diet program. Among my reasons for doing so are that I want to be and remain in good health. But an equally or even more strong reason is that I am disgusted with myself for being unfit and undisciplined. I see the regimen as a

---

[6]B. Williams, "Persons, Character and Morality", printed in *The Identities of Persons*, ed. A. Rorty, University of California Press, Berkeley, CA, 1976.

way of promoting my health and appearance but also and primarily as a way of contributing to my self-esteem, to realizing a conception of myself as disciplined with respect to my appetites. It is the results of my efforts in this latter respect that are especially important to me and what I value most about my success or failure. How I carry out the project makes a real difference to how I regard myself. For some people such a regimen is a matter of habit. They may have been trained in it as children or as athletes. For others it may be the sort of thing they go in for occasionally but not with any serious or sustained commitment. And to yet others it may seem silly, irrelevant, or not worth the effort. How the end figures in one's conception of himself is a subjective affair across persons and across time for the same person. The value of and commitment to the end are not straightforwardly consequences of its content. There may be some ends such that it appears there are reasons for *any* person to highly value them and be committed to them. We will come to this later. For now it is enough to point out that the presentation and even understanding of those reasons is not alone sufficient to drive those ends into one's set of motivational self-conceptions.[7]

An individual will typically have a constellation of these self-conceptions, rather than monomaniacal commitment to a single dominant one. That is surely possible, particularly if it is a rich and demanding one, like living a life of religious piety. But it is not typical. And we make adjustments and changes in these constellations, possibly even reversals, such as disavowing establishing world communism in favor of free enterprise and liberal politics.

What one's motivational self-conceptions are has a strong influence on one's patterns of reasoning and choosing an action overall. They put constraints on how she employs her resources and have implications for the worth and appropriateness of all sorts of possible activities and pursuits. We often evaluate the soundness of one's practical reasoning in terms of how it squares with one's professed primary ends. The latter supply criteria for whether one is being sincere or hypocritical or effective or ineffective in going about what he or she claims is important. Also, both in our own case and concerning others we judge how well suited or prepared, whether emotionally, intellectually, financially, and so forth, the individuals are to set about realizing their self-conceptions. Reasons of health, opportunity, natural talent, and so on can be mustered to encourage or dissuade. As these sorts of contingencies change their influence changes.

Additionally, one's motivational self-conceptions partially determine what one ought to be doing and why at future times. They typically involve

---

[7]I sketched out this theory of motivational self-conceptions and its relation to self-enjoyment and virtue in "The Place of Virtue in Happiness", in *Journal of Value Inquiry*, 19: 171–182, 1985. The presentation there is very compressed, but indicates the main theses developed here.

us in temporally-extended activities which may require doing many things in a particular order. Many of our activities will be linked, as when one seeks part-time work in order to pay for schooling in order to pursue a certain career. Through motivational self-conceptions we commit ourselves to patterns of motive, desire, explanation, and action. These may extend over long periods and be interlocking with other self-conceptions in ways that require a good deal of attention and thought. Also, it is because not all of a person's ends are given and fixed and because practical reason has a constructive employment that flattery, argument, and criticism can influence one's motivational self-conceptions.

The two special characteristics of these conceptions are that they express ends which one (a) desires for their own sake, and (b) judges to be worthwhile. These conditions are jointly satisfied by motivational self-conceptions and may be singly satisfied by other ends. Their joint satisfaction specifies the sense in which we *identify* with these conceptions; in which they are conceptions of self and not just ends.[8]

To call them self-conceptions is to say that through them one not only sees a way in which they do things but they supply the context of how one sees oneself. To say these ends are desired for their own sake marks the fact that they are not merely instrumental. They may be instrumental for someone else, or for me at a different time. But in those cases they are not the content of motivational self-conceptions. To say that they are judged to be worthwhile is to note the essentially normative aspect of the constructive activity of self-determination. Regarding these ends as worthwhile does not simply record the fact that one has certain desires, but that a judgment has been made. The worthwhileness of the ends is recognized on the basis of consideration, not just the strength of one's wants. Normative judgment is constitutive of deliberation and self-determination, not an optional supervenience. These conceptions are partially constitutive of the self. One's individuality is in part determined by the motivational self-conceptions that structure and direct thought and action in the respect that they are determinants of one's life history. Self-conceptions are not just beliefs about oneself or what one is doing, though people have these too. Nor are they ideals of what one would like or wishes for. A person can have these without being committed to their actually shaping his own thought and action. To have a given motivational self-conception is to commit and direct one's agency in a specific way. The activity in conformity with it just is the self in its practical aspect.

Many of the activities persons engage in are guided by concepts that do not jointly satisfy the two above-mentioned conditions. We may desire to drink a cup of coffee, not for its own sake, but only to stay awake in order

---

[8]My discussion here and in other places throughout this chapter has been influenced by Charles Taylor's "Responsibility For Self," in *The Identities of Persons*, ed. A. Rorty, University of California Press, Berkeley, CA, 1976.

to keep driving. We may think this a useful thing to do but not attach any worth to it apart from its instrumental value. We may even have reasons for otherwise regarding it as something not to be done. Or, for example, we may desire for its own sake to make a parachute jump out of an airplane, but not judge it to be worthwhile. And it is possible to regard something as worthwhile yet still not desire it for its own sake. Perhaps knowledge is something toward which many people have this attitude. It is acknowledged as a good thing in itself, but people just don't desire it for its own sake in an effective way. They are not genuinely committed to it. Where either or both conditions fail to be met the end is not one the agent identifies with or includes in his conception of what type of person he is. It is not a conception *through which* the self is partially constituted.

This notion of the self's being partially constituted by thought and action in conformity with self-conceptions is connected in an important way with the thesis that deliberation can be constructive. The activity of deliberation and settling upon an end may involve more than observing or acknowledging or looking for connections between propositions, maxims, and values. Sometimes these connections are brought about through the deliberative activity. Even if there are ready-made structures of practical reasoning available to employ, ways of going on and reasons to do so, the deliberative activity may be something quite different from examining and appropriating one of these structures or portions of them. In these cases one's authority and responsibility as an agent are more fully involved. A person may settle on a life plan, primary interests, and values very similar to those of others, even similar to those of others he knows. As a result, there is a fund of information, experience, and already-expended deliberative effort of those others available for him to exploit. It may, in certain respects, seem imprudent or inefficient not to exploit some of these resources. But the individual may feel a concern that he is not being adequately reflective, self-critical, and responsible in appropriating them. He may feel that his integrity requires him to "sort things out" for himself, not in ignorance of what is available to guide him, but also not being led along by it. What an outsider may regard as extra work is not so regarded by the person doing it. With respect to many of our specific ends and how we pursue them, what matters about them and how and why cannot be specified for us by others.

I have argued that the ends for persons are not fixed or given. It is chiefly in this respect that a personal life history differs from an organic life history. Both are end-oriented and teleologically structured. But persons experience openness with respect to ends. Their teleology is full fledged. Yet, I also want to argue that because a personal life history essentially involves thought and action in conformity with motivational self-conceptions, we can, *in a formal way,* characterize an end for persons, as such. That is, persons, by virtue of being persons have as an end that they should

desire for its own sake and judge to be worthwhile the exercise of their
capacities for thought and action. This end is that toward which the exercise for capacities in a personal life history is directed. I shall call this
condition of desiring for its own sake and finding worthwhile the exercise
of one's capacities *self-enjoyment*.[9]

    This notion of self-enjoyment is a good deal like Aristotle's notion of
happiness. It also involves an important relation to virtue. But I will not
start out by defining it to include virtue or any particular ends or activities.
The role of virtue in self-enjoyment is central. But we will work our way up
to it and not force any issues of moral psychology at the outset.

    That one's thought and action should be conducive toward self-enjoy-
ment is, so to speak, a regulative principle for a deliberating, end-setting,
being. The desire for self-enjoyment is a "master" motivation that directs
our exercise of our capacities by supplying a general end for them. This
does not entail that the pursuit of self-enjoyment is an activity other than
the specification and pursuit of specific ends. The pursuit of them under
certain conditions is *constitutive* of self-enjoyment. It is, I claim, a fact about
the nature of persons that they are motivated to pursue activities and ends
that they desire for their own sake. It is also a fact about them that they
engage in normative judgment about their ends and activities. This does
not imply that there are any specific ends that they necessarily desire for
their own sake or judge to be worthwhile. Rather, it belongs to the intrinsic
teleology of a personal life history that a person pursue ends with a view
toward self-enjoyment. Persons pursue self-enjoyment through striving to
realize motivational self-conceptions.[10]

    The notion of self-enjoyment has a good deal of explanatory signifi-
cance in accounting for how practical reason is employed. Consider why
people change their plans, cultivate new interests, adopt different
attitudes. Sometimes these changes are a result of persuasion, influence,
and altered circumstances. But they are also sometimes a function of a
deliberate re-orientation on the part of the individual. That is, these
changes are themselves a function of the exercise of capacities for self-
determination.

    It is not always irrational to undertake projects with a high risk of
failure or very high costs. It is not always irrational to engage oneself in
pursuits without full confidence in one's abilities and suitability. It *is* irrational to intentionally engage oneself in a manner that renders one misera-

[9]See R. Warner's "Enjoyment", in *Philosophical Review*, Vol. 89, No. 4, October 1980,
pp. 507–526. This is not an account of happiness or self-enjoyment, but it should be clear how
my account has been influenced by this work. See also his recent *Freedom, Enjoyment and
Happiness*, published by Cornell University Press, Ithaca, NY, 1987. I did not have the opportunity to benefit from that treatment of these topics before developing my own.

[10]See my "Deliberation, Self-Conceptions, and Self-Enjoyment" to appear in *Idealistic
Studies*, in Press. That piece is a condensed presentation of the main theses here about constructive practical reason and the intrinsic teleology of persons.

ble where this could be helped. Suffering is tolerable. Loss and failure are more or less inevitable. But the deliberate pursuit of misery is crazy. It does not *follow* from this that the guiding formal principle of practical reason is that it should conduce to self-enjoyment. But it is true that self-enjoyment is the "target" persons aim at. It is worthwhile to consider how a being who had to deliberate and choose, but who desired nothing for its own sake and made no normative judgments would go about organizing its life. There are in fact people who seem to fit this characterization at many points. But the combination of conditions is something they *suffer* and *suffer from*. They are either constitutionally defective on account of disease or injury or retardation, or perhaps they are severely depressed. They are somehow *incapacitated*. A being who was lacking by nature in the respects mentioned could survive, of course. I imagine many animals are just like that. But they are not creatures capable of acting for reasons, at least in the sense that persons are. My claim is that a being by its nature lacking in these respects is a non-person, even if it has some sort of psychology and we attribute beliefs and desires to it. It has no *self*.

A severely depressed person typically loses engagement with motivational self-conceptions and the pursuit of self-enjoyment. Their teleology is degraded into fatigue, boredom, and loss of interest. Things cease to matter as the constructive agency of the self is subverted. In some states of depression the constructive activity of the individual is so minimal and evaluative commitment to ends so weak that the person no longer even has natural and spontaneous emotional responses. How he or she feels about what happens seems not to matter. The person becomes an almost disinterested spectator of his or her own life, and fails to assimilate his or her own experiences fully and reflectively. These become phenomena which seem not to make any difference. This can reach a point beyond which the pursuit of self-enjoyment requires extraordinary effort. It can reach a point where the effort itself is regarded as not worthwhile. This sort of pathology is both cause and effect of debilitated capacity for constructive and evaluative practical activity. One is then in a condition of disordered rationality as well as emotionality, and this acts corrosively on the self. This is quite different from and much more pernicious than things going badly for someone. Sometimes depressed persons are even distrustful of the attempts by others to counsel or help and prefer instead a sort of indulgent negativity as if to confirm the desolation of their outlook. In some cases the acknowledgment of their contribution to their own misery can be therapeutic. They see that it is at least partly their own failing that is impeding them and undertake to bring down the barriers they confront or have erected. These people pursue a process of restoration of their capacities through self-motivated exercise of them, and can begin again to appreciate themselves.

It is just this appreciation of oneself through striving for self-enjoyment that non-persons are constitutionally incapable of, and the loss of which in persons is so painful and tragic. The idea that there is such a regulative, intrinsic end, for persons has been widely criticized and renounced. There are (at least) two major reasons for this. First, it is often thought that if there were such an intrinsic end there would be objective reasons that would compel any rational person to (a) see that it was so, and (b) pursue that end. But the loosening of an overambitious and idealized conception of rationality and the efficacy of appeals to it undermined that view. For example, Bernard Williams in *Morality* and in *Ethics and the Limits of Philosophy* has raised important objections to the idea that there is some privileged exercise of rationality in structuring and giving value to our lives. Even rational people disagree or suspend judgment about the deepest and most general issues: especially about the deepest and most general issues, whether theoretical or practical. And, as I have already urged, that there are reasons does not entail that anyone acts because there are those reasons to do so. The second reason is the gradual dissolution of the "metaphysical" and teleological theory of the nature of persons by mechanico-causal accounts, assimilable into the wider body of natural science. Many contemporary functionalist, materialist, and socio-biological theories are legatees of this scientific post-Enlightenment tradition.

That tradition has bred its own criticism and no longer dictates the acceptable categories of analysis of the problems. While much good explanation issued from it, it explained away too much. The knot of questions concerning the nature of persons, practical reason, moral value, and moral motivation still remains tied together. It is the notion of teleology that holds the whole thing together. We cannot give an illuminating, faithful account of practical reason without it, and we cannot capture and express the distinctive character of a personal life history without it. The remarks about depression were intended to illustrate the ill-effects of a disordered teleology. Without the notion of an overall regulative, formal characteristic for practical reason we cannot make good sense out of the distinctive activities of persons. To be a person is to be able to engage in certain types of activities, and while there is extensive openness in what these activities are, there are constraints determined by the capacities for them. The constraints are not just limitations; they are also structural and orienting principles. Self-determination is not a matter of overcoming these constraints but of constituting one's career through informing their plasticity. We don't choose to have self-enjoyment as an end. We choose what our self-enjoyment shall consist in. Without self-enjoyment as an end it is not clear why or how we should choose anything at all. Relative to other kinds of things persons are relatively impoverished in terms of instinct. This is not a defect. This is so because of the fact that the intrinsic end of persons is not something that could be realized through the action of instinct. Unless the action of striving to realize it is *constructive* activity it will not yield the appropriate result. The reason for this is that the core of self-enjoyment is enjoyment of being a purposive being. It is, in a sense not accessible to nonpersonal beings, our own causality that is enjoyed.

This is the main underlying fact that explains the rationality of changing one's activities, plans, and interests when they fail to conduce to self-enjoyment. The fact that it is one's own causality that is constitutive of the pursuit of self-enjoyment makes it both possible and necessary that self-determination contribute to it. One can wait for things to get better, hope for a change in circumstances, or rely on others for assistance, forbearance, and encouragement. But how these factors figure in the pursuit of self-enjoyment depends on the manner in which a person structures and orients his own thought and action. This activity is constructive in the sense that the individual determines the ordering of his powers for action and is not simply responding to conditions, including his own desires. We are best able to enjoy (in terms of stability and richness) what we bring about through our own power.

I realize that it may sound extreme or implausible that persons have as an intrinsic end the maximization of their self-determination. After all, as a plain matter of fact many people do not exert themselves in anything like an agency maximizing manner, and many people prefer passive or non-demanding pleasures to complex activities. But I believe the plausibility and correctness of this thesis can be indicated by describing its relation to some very general considerations about rationality. First, it hardly seems doubtful that it is rational to pursue a course in life that one finds desirable and worthwhile. This principle is not prejudiced in favor of any specific claims about just what is desirable and worthwhile. It is certain that many, many people are satisfied with enjoyments that do not require much deliberation, imagination, or conceptually articulate understanding. Thinkers such as Aristotle and even Mill are often accused of characterizing the pleasurable in a way that reflects the biases of the well-educated, socially aware, and intellectually energetic. I want this account to avoid that charge, and I believe it does. My point is not that some specific ends x, y, or z are necessarily in themselves more desirable or worthwhile ends than a, b, and c. Rather, I am making a more formal claim: that the stability and richness of enjoyment consequent upon an activity are related to the extent to which it *is* an activity in which the individual's various capacities are engaged. Perhaps most people prefer eating a terrific meal to preparing one, or knowing how to prepare one. But the enjoyment involved in the latter, because of the extensive involvement of abilities is typically a more extensive, enduring satisfaction. Of course there may also be such a thing as "knowing how" to enjoy a good meal, as opposed to just finding it delicious. But this is an illustration of and not a counterinstance to my point.

When I say that self-enjoyment crucially involves finding the exercise of one's causality naturally pleasing, I do not mean that people intentionally organize their lives with a view to maximizing their agency. That is an end obviously too remote and abstract to be action-guiding. What is motivationally action-guiding is how desirable and worthwhile one finds her undertakings. And there is a causal relation between the exercise of agency and the character of one's enjoyment that supplies a reason to engage in activities that put certain sorts of demands upon one's powers, including the sensitive, imaginative, deliberative, and so on. Activities in which one makes judgments and discriminations and regards what is going on with some measure of conceptual sophistication tend to yield superior enjoyment to more passive, less complexly engaging activities. My point is not that doing philology is better than baking holiday desserts. It is often a matter of the manner of engagement in the activity. For example, some people not only watch cricket and follow match results, they really find it interesting, while others find it an unintelligible bore that has the very rare distinction of being mysterious but not fascinating.

This claim about exercising agency is related to rationality because of how some highly general considerations about living pleasurable, worthwhile lives count as regulative principles for our deliberations and choices. We are best able to get what we want out of our lives by engaging our agency to ends we control through practical reason.

There is no guarantee of any sort that anyone will be successful in the pursuit of self-enjoyment. That does not render it any less an intrinsic end. It's just a fact about the world. We should observe, though, that *success* in the pursuit of ends one desires for their own sake and judges to be worthwhile is not a necessary condition for self-enjoyment. It is possible that *believing* one is successful will be sufficient. Suppose someone is devoted energetically and sincerely to finding a cure for a certain type of disease. These efforts may in fact be worthless, their approach all wrong. In ignorance of this the activity may still contribute to self-enjoyment. The more problematic sorts of cases are those in which self-deception is involved. Where agents' motivational self-conceptions involve them in pursuits that they correctly believe they cannot succeed in, or where they deny the truth of the fact that they are failing and yet proceed, they are not being tenacious but rather irrational. This is not always clear-cut. It may come to my attention that my researches are not yielding valuable results, but I press on anyway in the hope that a breakthrough is still possible. This and many other sorts of cases require a weighing of the evidence. Moreover, often one is not satisifed until he "finds out for himself". Someone may insist on pursuing a course as a mathematician, though that person seems to competent judges to lack the talent for it. A good deal of time and intellectual and psychological resources may need to be spent before the already available assessment of their talents is accepted. But to go on, not just inexpertly but incompetently would be foolish.

Self-deception, like depression, has effects that radiate out into rational, emotional, and psychological resources. It is disabling. It clouds judgment, interferes with sound reasoning, misleads, and requires a potentially exhausting effort to be sustained. Especially if it operates on a character trait it may result in hypocrisy. A person may deceive himself into thinking he is fairminded, though his actions belie this. One may find oneself furiously rationalizing both to oneself and to others. Expert and ambitious self-deception may survive being contradicted by the facts. But it leaves the individual always at risk of exposure. Self-esteem and confidence can be severely undermined when the veil of deception is torn down. Of course, this can ultimately be strongly to one's long-term advantage. But it invites guilt, shame, and, worse, self-contempt along the way. Responses of these kinds indicate the acknowledgement of the misuse of agency, of a failure of responsibility in the exercise of one's capacities.

Again, people can fail to realize successfully their motivational self-conceptions and know it without this subverting self-enjoyment. This is because it is the manner of employment of their agency that is desired for its own sake and judged to be worthwhile. Success in *striving to realize* must be distinguished from *successfully achieving*. Moreover, people may succeed in realizing their motivational self-conceptions without achieving self-enjoyment. We sometimes find, as we say, that "things are not all they were cracked up to be." We can be disappointed even in success. This disappointment is a sufficient reason to make changes in the relevant self-conceptions.

The most stable condition is that in which striving to realize motivational self-conceptions continuously yields self-enjoyment in a way that continues to supply a reason to go on in the same manner. Self-enjoyment is not restricted to the condition of *completed* realization of motivational self-conceptions. Not only is it achievable in the process of striving to realize them, but motivational self-conceptions may be of the type that have no well-defined point of completed realization. I shall argue later that being virtuous is like that. But there are many other such ends as well. The pursuit of certain kinds of knowledge or aesthetic experiences is never completed. But their incompleteness does not imply lack of success or that they are not fulfilling. Finding an activity to be desirable for its own sake and worthwhile is to acknowledge an enjoyment-generated reason to continue engagement in it. It is not necessarily augmented by being brought to a specific stage of completion.

I remarked earlier that which particular ends and activities meet the conditions for self-enjoyment is a subjective affair, varying across individuals, and also that self-enjoyment typically involves engagement with a number of harmonious ends. Individuals must make decisions about planning and scheduling. We can at least imagine someone having not only a dominant motivational self-conception but a monomaniacal one. For example, at the outside limits of plausibility we can imagine someone deriving self-enjoyment from imagining over and over again all of the playing cards in a normal deck. But this seems to us such an impoverished end, so uninteresting, because it requires so few of one's capacities. As Rawls has expressed the point:

> Other things equal, human beings enjoy the exercise of their realized capacities (their innate and trained abilities), and the enjoyment increases the more the capacity is realized, or the greater its complexity. The intuitive idea here is that human beings take more pleasure in doing something as they become more proficient at it, and of two activities they do equally well, they prefer the one calling on a larger repertoire of more intricate and subtle discriminations.[11]

This seems to me a quite general, though perhaps not necessary truth, about persons attested to even by activities such as watching a sports competition. Greater understanding of the game helps one to enjoy it more fully, the understanding and enjoyment often put together under the heading of "appreciation." A monomaniacal end like playing card-imagining is likely to quickly exhaust its potential for yielding enjoyment. There is nothing intrinsically wrong with it. The point here is that while there is not a law-like relation of strict proportionality, there is a causal explanatory relation between degrees of complexity of exercise of one's capacities for self-determination and achievement of self-enjoyment. We can say that there is a prima facie presumption of rationality in favor of pursuing a number of harmonious, complementary ends which can be pursued over an extended period and in varying circumstances.[12]

Rawls calls this view that the exercise of capacities conduces to enjoyment and the enjoyment increases with the complexity of activity the Aristotelian Principle. Like him, I see it as a principle of motivation. He also connects it to the psychology of self-esteem and securing the admiration of others. In describing the relation of the Principle to forming and executing a rational life-plan he says:

> A rational plan—constrained as always by the principles of right—allows a person to flourish, so far as circumstances permit, and to exercise his realized abilities as much as he can. Moreover, his fellow associates are likely to sup-

[11]J. Rawls, *A Theory of Justice*, Harvard University Press, Cambridge, MA, 1971, p. 426.

[12]Rawls discusses this sort of case on pages 432 and 433 of *A Theory of Justice*. In describing someone whose only pleasure is counting blades of grass in certain geometrically shaped areas such as park squares and well-trimmed lawns, he says:

> I mention this fanciful case only to show that the correctness of the definition of a person's good in terms of the rational plan for him does not require the truth of the Aristotelian Principle. The definition is satisfactory, I believe, even if this principle should prove inaccurate, or fail altogether. But by assuming the principle we seem to be able to account for what things are recognized as good for human beings taking them as they are.

port these activities as promoting the common interest and also to take pleasure in them as displays of human excellence. To the degree, then, that the
esteem and admiration of others is desired, the activities favored by the
Aristotelian Principle are good for other persons as well.[13]

He also notes that carrying out a life plan in accordance with the Aristotelian Principle supports and augments self-esteem in that it involves
engagement in activities one judges to be worthwhile and believes are
within one's capabilities. The present account has much the same contours
in the way it relates agency to enjoyment and a person's conception of the
worth of his or her activities and life.[14]

Moreover, there are broad, more or less commonsensical considerations about the rationality of the relation of means to ends and the com-
patibility of different ends. One typically cannot simultaneously train full-
time for Olympic trials and go to medical school. And it may be difficult to
judge what kinds of interests and activities will yield self-enjoyment. There
are the obvious facts that some people seek out adventure, risk, and novelty, while others would never consider it. Friends and family members
often surprise us with decisions and changes of heart and mind about their
commitments and primary concerns. Family history, the attitudes of
society, and availability of various sorts of resources all bear on how we
advise others, judge their activities, and understand what they are about.
We are no longer particularly inclined to send our sons off to monasteries;
and the rich no longer buy commissions in the military. Social, economic,
and cultural changes reshape what is thinkable, possible, and regarded as
responsible with respect to life plans. Indeed, the pursuit of self-enjoyment
through striving to realize certain self-conceptions is punishable by social
censure, fines, imprisonment, and even death.

Self-determination is subject to many different influences all the time
and in a rich variety of ways. Criteria that one employs in practical reasoning are often not chosen. They are a result of forces and factors one may
not even be aware of. Many of them, deliberately or not, even have the
effect of undermining self-determination. Subtle coercion, even when not
recognized as such by the practitioner, is a pervasive fact of life. Moreover,
a person whose life has been shaped and directed by others is not incapable
of self-enjoyment, though it is a familiar fact of life that interference with
self-determination can frustrate the achievement of self-enjoyment even
where the interference is well-intentioned. One man's altruism may be
another man's paternalism.

But within the complex manifold of influences and forces that operate on someone, the fundamental and distinctive fact about persons is that
they have the capacity for self-determination, for internally-motivated,

---

[13]J. Rawls, *A Theory of Justice*, Harvard University Press, Cambridge, MA, 1971, p. 429.
[14]Rawls's discussion of these points is primarily in section 67 of *A Theory of Justice*.

internally-directed activity. Even if a person takes the line of least resistance and does not go in for reflective, self-critical consideration of his plans, values and interests, he is nonetheless a self-determining individual. He just does not exercise the capacities for self-determination as fully as he might. A standard objection to this sort of view is that many people just do not have those capacities, or that none of us does. Perhaps we can sometimes do what we please but really, what we please is in the end not something we exercise any power over. One's character and outlook are shaped and oriented by the natural and social world, and whatever intervention one makes in how things are going anyway has an explanation that does *not* refer to any special powers of initiation on the part of so-called agency.

As an initial observation on this view, consider two pairs of distinctions. The first is the distinction between character in the descriptive sense and character in the normative sense, and the second, the distinction between shallowness of character and being a victim of compulsion. Consider the first distinction. Everyone has a character in the descriptive sense, in the neutral sense of having a collection of personal traits. Some people also have character in the normative sense that they are reflective, exercise care in judgment, and are concerned for what differences their actions and attitudes and the acts and attitudes of others make. Or, conversely, we might say "yes, he has a good deal of character, but all bad." Character is not only simple or complex, dynamic or dull, and so forth. It is also dignified or not, admirable or not, even serious or not. Much of our normative consideration of someone's character has to do with what the individual himself imparts to it. A shallow character is typically regarded as one produced by a minimum of constructive activity. The person does not exercise authority over himself, take himself seriously in certain ways. He is not as fully concerned with his own responsibility for what he is like as we believe he ought to be. This is not to say that he is not serious about what he does or is an irresponsible person. Rather, he lacks a measure of depth concerning himself and we might say is not serious *as* a person. He needn't be reckless or insincere or self-centered. But he does not raise and confront basic questions of value and of the significance and motivations of his actions and attitudes. His own character is not something he reasons about and judges with much care.

If someone is shallow in this way we adopt different attitudes toward him than if his actions and motivations are more completely the product of forces he cannot control. Even upbringing and indoctrination and socialization can be as powerfully coercive as addiction or psychological disorders. Each can reach a point where they are irresistible. But typically people are not victims of irresistible forces of these kinds. And even sometimes where they are it is their own fault by virtue of their willingly submitting. We might note here a distinction between self-control and self-mastery. The genuine victim of compulsion is not in control of himself and

The genuine victim of compulsion is not in control of himself and so is incapable of self-mastery, of fully effective self-determination. The shallow character, the individual who forfeits self-mastery in favor of lesser exertions of self-determination is still in control of himself. It is important to note the difference between lack of self-determination on account of an undermining cause operating on it, and lack of it on account of failure to exercise it. A habit of the second type can come to be as debilitating as a cause of the first type, though one is a failing where the other is not.

Agency is not a cause which is simply "on" of "off." This is perhaps why it has been so difficult for generations of philosophers to formulate necessary and sufficient conditions for "x acts freely . . . ." These formulations have often exhibited a good deal more ingenuity than insight, and the failure to arrive at a satisfactory account has frequently prompted the response that there just is not any self-determination. I think the view that sees the phenomenon most clearly is that self-determination is a matter of degree. Some people exercise it more than others. Like other capacities, it can be developed or stunted, strengthened or weakened. And, like many other capacities, the degree to which it *can* be effectively exercised partially depends upon how much it *is* effectively exercised. Controlling one's appetites for example, can become easier by virtue of one's becoming disposed that way through effort and resolve. What one can "help" or not "help" or at least the effort required, often depends in part on the character of dispositions of certain sorts that the person has brought about in himself. The strength of the temptation is not solely a function of the object. It depends also on how the desire figures in an economy of thought, interest, motive, and action that the individual has established or is trying to establish in himself. That economy is influenced and constrained but not determined by non-agent causes. It has been one of the main points of the discussion so far that what it is to be a person necessitates the constructive activity of establishing some such economy.

Even where the constructive work is minimal, and the person is shaped by others, circumstances, and unreflective adoption of ends and attitudes he is still to a high degree responsible for himself. Yielding to such influences is rarely a conscious choice. But the lack of deliberation and choice does not imply a proportionate lack of responsibility. It is still true that to an extent the character of one's life history is self-imposed, in that the determinants of it are appropriated though without question, resistance, or criticism. Granted, there are circumstances that may be present throughout one's life in which such activities are not genuine practical possibilities and it is true that influencing factors are present to a degree in everyone's life. But these considerations note the limitations on responsibility for oneself. They do not explain it away.

I remarked earlier that we are not mere observers of our practical activities. The self as a cause is what it does. This involves second-order or higher-order awareness. But the constructive activity of deliberation and the engagement with motivational self-conceptions are not just processes happening in one. I identify with them in the respect that they are the exercises of certain capacities constitutive of me. They are not in me as freight is in a ship, to counterfeit a phrase. While it is a contingent matter what motivational self-conceptions I have, my conception of myself, of my individuality is not detachable from them. They partially constitute the material that goes into the appreciation of myself as *this* individual having *this* life history proceeding in *this* unique way. I can imagine things having gone differently, leading my life otherwise, and having had different goals, interests, and values. But the perspective from which I can do such things is not a neutral, purely observational one. It is informed and textured by the choices, commitments, and attitudes that I have actually made and adopted. What appear to me as genuine practical alternatives, things I could have done or may do in the future, and the sorts of reasons for them have a character largely influenced by the character of my history of self-determination. Notions of what could have or may fit into my life history are attached to a locus of projection that is to a significant extent of my own making.

Chapter 2

Unity and Historical Self-Conceptions

The causality of agency is not just choice or initiation, it is also constructive activity. The teleology of persons requires this. We are all, in a sense, self-made men. The constructive activity characterized so far is primarily first order. It is the activity through which we each determine our thought and action and trace out a particular life history. The teleological form of this history of activity is that it should conduce to self-enjoyment.

In addition to this first-order history of choices, reasonings, attitudes, and plans is a second-order history, a history *of* them. The *unity* of a personal life history is constructed by the individual who has it. Unity is self-imposed by means of the individual's producing for himself an interpretive, explanatory historical self-conception. This conception, which I call a *personal narrative* is not an optional supervenience on the first-order self-conceptions. It is an intrinsic component of a personal history and as fully an exercise of the teleology of persons as commitment to motivational self-conceptions. We think of our lives in the category of unity and rarely have the occasion or interest to exercise ourselves very much about identity. The latter is more nearly a distinctively philosophical issue and routinely receives formal/causal explication. Identity and unity are closely linked, though neither is simply a consequence of the other. Actual memory connectedness is a necessary condition for unity. But it supplies matter that is informed by a self-imposed construction, and supplies only part of the matter. The unifying account embraces past, present, and future, and so includes constituents that go beyond what is given by memory. Moreover, it is not just a record of memory. It is an interpretive representation of oneself, and not just an awareness of continuity.[1] I will not attempt to supply an account of personal identity here as a background for or complement to the account of unity. The latter should make plain how closely integrated they are, but it can also be discussed independently.

I introduced the notion of representation earlier by way of criticizing functional accounts of life histories, whether organic or personal. It is my view that the teleology of a life history involves representation of future states. I will not argue a case for this in the biological context, where such an argument is clearly necessary. I do not think it is necessary in the context of persons. It is clear that we represent to ourselves not only possible future states but past states (both possible and actual) as well. Actual memory connectedness is one species of representing the past. Intentionality and expectation are species of representation of the future. The main thrust of my claims here is that a personal narrative is a special representation of one's history. It brings together into a coherent, followable whole representations of past, present, and future, in which motivational self-conceptions have a focal place. A personal narrative is, in large part, a history of motivational self-conceptions and the striving to realize them. It is an accounting to oneself of oneself, not just as a record but as an articulation of a perspective on one's past and an orientation toward the future.

There has been considerable discussion of the importance of the past in issues concerning identity, the shaping of character, and the transmission of influence of past experiences. But much of the significance of the past, the record supplied by memory, its interpretation, and the transmission of influence has to do with how it is related to one's conception of the future. One's past, present, and future are linked in a single complex representation of a life history. The past matters to us not just for what it supplies but also, in our consideration of it, what it *indicates*. It is through reflection on the past that we can inform and instruct ourselves about what our dispositions, abilities, and typical responses and attitudes are. It gives us a conception of what we can do, need to do, and so forth.

These representations of ourselves to ourselves may be accurate or not, honest or not, detailed or not, and so on. We will discuss some of the more important dysfunctions later on. Here it is enough to note how dependent people are on their historical self-conceptions in understanding their past and reasoning about how to proceed. As the account of this develops I will argue that having the right sort of personal narrative con-

---

[1]See my "The Idea of a Personal History", *International Philosophical Quarterly*, June 1984, pp. 179–187.

duces to self-enjoyment, because of the contribution it makes to effective self-determination. I shall argue that self-knowledge contributes to self-enjoyment both as a cause and a constituent.

Historical self-knowledge takes the form of a narrative in that it involves fitting together, integrating into a unified followable whole representations of past, present, and future. A narrative is a story, and I take it that the essential element of a story is *followability*. W. B. Gallie, in *Philosophy & The Historical Understanding* puts this point as follows:

> Following a story. . . is a teleologically guided form of attention. We are pulled along by our sympathies toward a promised yet always open conclusion, across any number of contingent, surprising events, but always on the understanding that these will not divert us hopelessly from the vaguely promised end.[2]

His two main theses about what a story is are that (1) "The crucial developments in any story are essentially contingent" and (2) "The act of following such developments depends upon their human interest. . . ."[3] A story develops through the very contingencies that compose it and their being ordered and related in ways that sustain our interest. The interest that one has in his own personal narrative has a special type of exigency, since it is the story of one's own life. It is a story that the individual constructs and identifies with, and its episodes of joy, success, failure, action, and suffering have an immediacy and influence that are unique.

It is of course chiefly through memory that we have access to our past. But through memory we do more than merely report what has gone before. Engagement with the past can be much more complete and involved than that, including elements of reconstruction, evaluation, and interpretation. A personal narrative is a critical history.

While the past is closed in the respect that nothing more can happen in it we can still look back and reflect on prior experiences of openness and opportunity. We can judge our earlier motives, rethink past deliberations, and evaluate past situations. We can judge how and why things mattered to us, what difference it has made, and how this understanding influences our views of the present and future. In reflectively assessing past experiences we often not only report to ourselves what we thought and felt but also try to integrate the episode and our appreciation of it into an overall conception of our lives. For example, one might think back upon a failed romance and sort out how its impact radiated into a broad range of concerns and decisions, and how one's reactions influenced attitudes toward oneself and various other people and issues. The recollection may be emo-

---

[2] W. B. Gallie, *Philosophy & the Historical Understanding*, Schocken Books, New York, 1964, pp. 64–65.

[3] Ibid, p. 48.

tionally charged and attended by pleasure or pain. Even if the episode is no longer a "live issue" its significance endures. A traumatic experience can become an exaggerated focus for one's energies and outlook and later be relegated to a less central and demanding role, though its influence is still important. We might think "Thank God I've gotten over that," or "I really did not have a realistic conception of what I should have been doing." Recollection can be broadened and deepened into imaginative reconstruction accompanied by interpretation of the import of the past for what one thinks and does and plans and desires.[4] Our awareness and appreciation of our past is not merely observational; it involves activity. It is an exercise of agency just as projection into the future is.

The self as a cause informs and mediates the past accessible to it through actual memory connectedness. There are constraints over how much of the past is accessible; there are causal factors we do not control. But there is also a sense in which the past is made or constructed through present activity. As a consequence, people are responsible to an extent for their conception of the past. Much of this responsibility has to do with how the influence of past experience is regarded and assimilated. Psychological defenses can distort and disguise the past but its influence will not be altogether suppressed. These defenses alter but do not destroy what they are worked upon.

For example, consider an individual who never fully "amounted to" what he wanted to. Not that some specific plan or end was frustrated, but that he never felt satisfied with his accomplishments. He is able to live decently, raise a family comfortably, and live without deprivation or suffering. All of this he manages with much hard work and struggle, and to observers he appears to have exerted himself and done well, but he has gnawing feelings of inadequacy. Perhaps early hardships and uncertainties and lack of resources forced him to lower his expectations and curtail his aspirations. While there had been no specific accomplishment that he regarded as a primary or overriding goal, he still feels as if his successes had been stunted, incomplete, that if given better opportunities he could have "gone on to better things." He feels somewhat victimized and his frustration is vented as anger. It is not anger at any particular persons or events, but just his circumstances in general as though they conspired to thwart him. It is not so much that he never had the wealth or public recognition he desired but that he feels his own capacities have been impeded and channeled away from their full development. He is not satisfied with any of his successes and regards them as partial. He feels as though he has been forced to devote his energies to lesser undertakings

---

[4]See R. Wollheim's "On Persons and Their Lives," in *Explaining Emotions*, ed. A. Rorty, University of California Press, Berkeley, CA, 1980, for a discussion of the transmission of influence of past experiences.

than what they warranted, that what he has been occupied in has been beneath him.

This sort of attitude and its accompanying anger may be the result of exaggerated youthful self-conceptions. This may be the product of familial influences, of being convinced early that one "will go far" or "do great things" or they may be the result of constantly feeling that opportunities were denied by the force of circumstances. This man feels as though he never became what he could have been. His frustration becomes cynical, bitter, and envious. He substitutes negativism toward others for self-esteem and regards his cynicism as the virtue of perceiving that others are not as capable and talented as he. He vents his dissatisfaction with himself as contempt for others.

One plausible way to regard this individual's outlook is that he never succeeded in reconciling himself to limitations that were unavoidable. They may have been internal. Perhaps his standards for himself were unrealistic. But whether or not that is so or could ever be known to be so, the chief point here is that he cultivates an unrealistic and overly critical attitude toward others, perhaps even loved ones whom he regards as drawing too much on him and constraining him. He may never express this openly, but his bitterness reveals it.

As time passes and his frustration becomes more firmly entrenched he comes more and more to see himself as having been denied. He can easily interpret his past to conform to this theme and interpret the denial as having been imposed upon him, as an injustice. This becomes the dominant notion of his understanding of his past. To an extent it may be true. But he elevates it to the level of an encompassing theory of his life. It becomes so entrenched that he is psychologically unable, because unwilling, to consider that his expectations outran his exertions, or that they were unrealistic. That is, he sees what is really internal conflict as conflict with externals. Never having adequately adjusted his sense of himself and his importance to the way the world is, he blames the world for failing to properly acknowledge him. This failure on his part and his interpretation of it undermines his ability to achieve self-enjoyment. He may even enthusiastically indulge his bitterness as a substitute for re-examining himself. In this sort of case not only is there transmission of influence of past experiences, but the influence is strengthened as the unifying pressure of the individual's account of his life increases in a particular direction.

While an observer may think that this individual is being unfair to both himself and others, he regards the perspective that informs his personal narrative as essential to it and crucial to a coherent, unified conception of his history. The passage of time allows him to reinforce this perspective and even alter his own earlier conceptions of his history to fit it. What we interpret as distorting and inaccurate he regards as realistic and well confirmed. He is secure in his self-persuasion, to the point where such persuasion becomes a readily supplied need.

This example illustrates two points. First, that psychological and attitudinal needs can significantly influence a personal narrative. A kind of personal ideology can have an extensively distorting effect. Second, that there are no general, specifiable limits on revision of a personal narrative. Components may be more or less given by memory. But how they are fitted together and interpreted is not a matter that is given or fixed. How someone thinks of his adolescence when he is twenty is bound to be quite different from how he thinks of his adolescence when he is thirty-five or sixty. Changes in the present motivate changes in our conceptions of our past as well as the future. The agency of self-consciousness extends both backward and forward in time in the activity of constituting unity.

As I have argued, the unity of a personal life history is not something we strive to discover. We constitute it. At the same time the past delivers much of itself through memory and the transmission of influences that shape character, outlook, motives and so on. Past experiences have effects on emotionality. Past choices and actions have effects on present ones and so on. Denial of the past and its influence reshapes but does not erase them. That the past influences the present and one's self-conceptions is not optional. It is in the manner that it does so that the constructive power of agency can be effective. How we address and engage with the past partially determines what its influence and significance will be.

The place of motivational self-conceptions is particularly significant in the construction of a personal narrative. The account one supplies to oneself of the adoption of and commitment to them will be in large part a history of one's agency. It will be the account of the individual's striving to realize the intrinsic teleology of personhood in the manner peculiar to him. Through appreciation of one's motivational self-conceptions the individual achieves an appreciation of how, why, and to what extent he has exercised authority over and responsibility for himself. The account of motivational self-conceptions is not detachable from the rest of the content of one's past. The influences of others, of experiences, circumstances, emotionality, psychological make-up, and so on are all inextricably bound-up together. But the account of motivational self-conceptions will indicate how one's capacities for self-determination have been exercised and how one's own causality has figured in the determination of his life history. This kind of understanding is crucial to continued, effective exercise of self-determination. R. G. Collingwood has expressed the significance of historical understanding as follows:

> History is 'for' human self-knowledge. . . knowing yourself means knowing, first what it is to be a man; secondly knowing what it is to be the kind of man

you are; and thirdly, knowing what it is to be the man *you* are and nobody else is. Knowing yourself means knowing what you can do; and since nobody knows what he can do until he tries; the only clue to what man can do is what man has done. The value of history, then, is that it teaches us what man has done and thus what man is.[5]

A person can ignore, suppress, falsify, or deny the past. But in so doing he distorts the information and instruction that it offers and corrupts his present conception of himself. Knowledge of one's abilities, inclinations, and attitudes is possible only through assimilation of and engagement with the past. Failure at this undermines the causality of agency. The latter is facilitated by an understanding of its operation, even if this understanding shows it to be interfered with and diminished by factors external to it. Lack of understanding of one's own causality reinforces the limitations upon it. As argued earlier, self-determination is not a power that is simply on or off or that can be turned on or off. It can be degraded by ignorance of its prior operations. A person can render himself relatively unfree through failure to exercise this power or by allowing other causal influences to increase their efficacy, including ignorance of himself.

For example, an experience that causes a great deal of mental suffering can become an exaggerated focus of concern and anxiety, and in that respect be debilitating. Some shameful past episode may so thoroughly haunt that there is an almost perverse desire to relive, revivify, and linger over it. The guilt and remorse become objects of indulgence. Instead of learning from the experience, or assimilating it in a manner in which it is accepted but not continuously gnawing at one's self-esteem, it is brought again and again to the forefront of self-examination. One may even allow its influence to spread and begin to interpret other episodes and experiences accordingly. Even as one realizes how important it is to "get over" the effects of the experience, it presses without resistance further into the individual's view of himself. If this process goes even further, the person can actually undermine his self-worth so much as to invite contempt, as though to do so were to confirm what the individual thought about himself all along. This sort of disorder is not merely psychological. It is a moral disorder: moral because of how agency and one's responsibility figure in its etiology. It is invited and encouraged, not just because of the agent's initial responsibility in its source, but because of how its influence is managed. There may well be a much longer, more complicated story about why this person goes in for this sort of seemingly deliberate psychological and emotional self-abuse, a story that involves other people and their conceptions of themselves and this person. But this is a sort of internal conflict that a

<hr>

[5] R. G. Collingwood, *The Idea of History,* ed. T. M. Knox, Oxford University Press, New York, 1956, p. 10.

person has, to a large extent, the ability and responsibility to come to terms with. Especially when it is realized how deleterious the effects are of the kind of failure described, one comes to understand that there is a good reason to prevail over their causes. Otherwise they operate in opposition to the capacity for self-determination rather than contributing to a fuller understanding of it. Very often guilt, shame, and remorse and the like are rational and appropriate responses to one's thought and action. But there are rational and appropriate responses to them as well.

The same is true of an emotion such as sadness, even where the cause does not involve the individual's responsibility. Sadness at the loss of a loved one, for example, can become a consuming preoccupation. Sometimes the more sad we become the more we almost wish to be sad, as though we welcome the flood of emotion and our sinking in it. People will cling to sadness with a kind of proprietary attitude, as though to help them out of it were insulting or intrusive. To a point this may be an appropriate response. The experience cannot be assimilated if we are encouraged or inclined to suppress it, deny its strength or reality, or inhibit giving expression to our emotions. But beyond that point, occupation with it is indicative of failure to assimilate it successfully. Persons can even come to see their lot in life as pitiful, as a kind of rationalization and excuse for not coming to terms with their grief. This can involve notions of the unreality or unimportance of the present or future. It can involve disengagement from people and activities or unwillingness to take initiatives or even promote one's own well-being, as if all of one's interests have been undermined and dissolved. Sometimes this can lead to a kind of salutary crisis of emotional reorientation. But it can also be crippling.

How we represent or misrepresent the past influences how we represent the present and future. This is because the character of interpretation involves thematic unity, not just the aggregative inclusion of episodes. An unrealistic, fantastic, self-deceiving conception of the past will retain those attributes in our projection of ourselves into the future. We develop habits of interpretation that are no more easy to break than habits of behavior, even in the knowledge that they are bad habits. As I remarked earlier, habits of interpretation are not always chosen. They may well have an explanation that refers to all sorts of causes beyond the agency of the individual. But there is yet a sense in which the individual is responsible for them. Psychological motives for seeing oneself in certain ways are themselves possible objects of interpretive representation. In discussing the interpretation of motives and evaluations, Charles Taylor writes:

> There are more or less adequate, more or less truthful, more self-clairvoyant or self-deluding interpretations. Because of this double fact, because an articulation can be *wrong*, and yet it shapes what it is wrong about, we sometimes

see erroneous articulations as involving a distortion of the reality concerned. We don't just speak of error but frequently also of illusion or delusion.[6]

Developing or articulating an understanding of one's history is not primarily a matter of gathering and organizing information. Not just the import of the "facts" but the "facts" themselves are not always self-presenting. This sort of understanding is something we construct, but not without any constraints or controls. It can be done well or badly.

Accurate representation is facilitated by self-determination. My claim here is that one's own agency is more fully and readily understood as a cause than the operation of other causes. One's own causality is maximally intelligible in understanding and unifying a personal history. The more of my own causality that I impart to my career, the more transparent the determination of it. It is my own authority and responsibility that I apprehend and penetrate. These are better known to me than other causes because they just are what I constitute them to be. The more my constructive agency is involved in motivational self-conceptions the more I can fully appreciate their character. We are less liable to error or illusion about our agency than about other causes. This is because it is not just something going on in or happening to me. It just is me in self-conscious practical engagement. Other causes may be no less vivid and obviously present. But they are not what I make them. *They* have a history which I do not determine.

These considerations about understanding the past portion of a personal history apply to the future as well. In settling upon a course of action and making decisions and plans I can try to sort out the role of my agency from other factors. I may not do this, and may simply go on along a line of least resistance without much critical reflection. I may take the issue of what ends and values to identify with and commit to as more or less settled. But if I don't, self-determination is involved to the extent that I select and organize them. Because I initiate and sustain the constructive dimension of deliberation its motive and character are most fully accessible to my understanding.

Concern about having historical self-knowledge is an interest in the self that we have because we acknowledge ourselves as self-determining. The answer to the question "How have I led my life?" is part of the answer to the question "What sort of person am I and why?" Illusion, fantasy, and falsification can be involved in the answer to either of these, but if they are excluded, we will then be able to produce an accurate representation of the past. The more my agency has determined my history the less effort is required to represent it accurately. It is, to that extent, self-disclosing and the interest in it will be correspondingly satisfied. Difficulties in satisfying

[6]C. Taylor, "Responsibility for Self," in *The Identities of Persons*, ed. A. Rorty, University of California Press, Berkeley, CA, 1976, p. 296.

that interest are a result of the opacity of non-agent causes. When one acts through agency, understanding the motive and character of the act is present in it. These properties of it do not need to be "looked into".

People are sometimes content to forego any particularly reflective, detailed, or evaluative historical self-knowledge. They may even be satisfied with a simplistic second-order self-conception such as "I'm a drinking man", or "I devote myself solely and completely to the service of the state." Such one-liners may even have a hard grain of truth in them. But they too have some sort of explanation. Lack of interest in the explanation of one's history strikes us as a kind of shallowness or lack of character. This is because of the relations between self-determination and self-knowledge. Not to be concerned with the latter is symptomatic of unconcern with the former. And this is indicative of a lack of seriousness and criticism with respect to the ground, import, and effects of one's actions. We might worry about how seriously this sort of person takes others. Why and how he came to be a drinking man and what he thinks of it matters to us in so far as it influences what attitudes toward him are appropriate. Casanova, for example, says of himself in his *Memoirs*:

> The chief business of my life has always been to indulge my senses; I never knew anything of greater importance. I felt myself born for the fair sex. I have ever loved it dearly, and I have been loved by it as often and as much as I could. I have likewise always had a great weakness for good living, and I ever felt passionately fond of every new object which excited my curiosity.[7]

Casanova was not *merely* a dissipated seducer and vice-merchant. We can find him objectionable in many ways, but not quite contemptible. His life history easily motivates sympathy and even envy in a way that the story of a man who simply pursues food and sex does not. Casanova at least had a kind of aesthetic appreciation and honest and articulate conception of what he had committed himself to. This is not true of someone who just consistently and selfishly seeks sensual gratification.

For the individual who conceptualizes her life history through a simplistic, unreflective theme, her history is just a series being added to without critical, evaluative engagement with the future. She does not strive to project herself except as "going on." This can, of course, be the situation of someone in awful circumstances that effectively close off the openness she would otherwise enjoy. Deprivation, coercion, and other factors can idle the teleology of persons, so that there is almost literally nothing to look forward to, at least under one's own control. But this sort of closure is imposed upon a person from without. It is circumstantial, even if it results in permanent debility of the person. It is an obviously different sort of case

---

[7]J. Casanova, *The Memoirs of Jacques Casanova*, ed. L. Levinson, New York, Macmillan, 1962.

than where the closure is the result of choice: where it flows from, rather than determines, the individual character.

These remarks are not intended to suggest that depth of character or taking oneself seriously requires constant consideration of alternative futures and reevaluation of one's plans and interests. The situation here is analogous to the past-regarding situation. What is admirable and desirable is a careful, articulate, critical appreciation that is free from self-deception and dogma. A critical attitude toward one's life history may no more lead to dramatic revisions in how one proceeds into the future than critical appraisal of a scientific theory will automatically lead to its abandonment. Rather, it may reveal excellent reasons to continue to explain and understand in accordance with it.

The type of both forward-looking and backward-looking constructive activity I have described need not be something one stops other activities to do. This can occasionally be the case where particular perplexities and concerns are felt. But ordinarily it is just a dimension of how one sees oneself and how one leads one's life. It is not one item on a list of things one does, or an activity that needs to be fitted into a broader schedule of activities. It may get this specific focus in times of trauma or in therapeutic contexts. But ordinarily people no more need to stop and prepare answers to questions about how they view themselves, than they must do that to answer the question "what are you doing?" This is because people identify with at least some sort of historical self-conception. Even if they find themselves going on at great length and in much detail, telling the story of their lives or some portion of them, this usually does not need preparation. In a conversation, particularly with someone you trust, or in a time of emotional need, the story just "comes out," flows, though along the way, or later on, it may be changed. I would imagine that the story of the past generally flows more easily than that of the future, just because the facts and details are already there. People may strongly identify with a conception of how they wish to carry on in the future and have a good idea of what to expect. But the future is indeterminate in a way that the past can never be.

The past can be reinterpreted, and a person may never settle on a fixed version of his or her past. But the future as we conceive it can literally be remade, perhaps through gradual, incremental alterations, perhaps through a radical and deep-cutting change. In either case it is continuous with the past and it is to the past that we must often look for a large part of the explanation of changed conceptions of the future. Even seemingly drastic discontinuities, conversions of one or another sort, arise out of whatever version of the past we hold. If someone changes the meaning of his or her life through adoption of completely changed motivational self-conceptions, the past, present, and future are not thereby rendered incommensurable. The changes in meaning are grounded in a stability of reference, the self, the individual to and in which they occur. Even in making a claim such as "I'm a different person now than I was then" it is understood that the significance of this, what is either wonderful or awful about it, is that this is the same person. The remark is an expression of how greatly a person can change or be changed without ceasing to be the same individual. It is the fact of unity that makes such changes so remarkable.

Persons typically value and strive for self-imposed unity and have a good reason to *because* they are self-determining. A person is an entity with identity but who must in a crucial sense constitute his individuality. I do not mean this metaphysically. The entity which is a person is individuated just in its being some kind of entity, a human being. But bodily persistence and the capacity for temporally extended mental connectedness are prerequisites for personal individuality that do not of their own exhaust what individuality is. The type of individuality I am speaking of here is defined by an answer to the question, "What have I made of myself?"

Lack of unity can lead to confusion, conflict, and a diffracted awareness and appreciation of what one can do and the character and causality of one's actions. This is not an inevitable result. It may even be a result that the individual is not conscious of. A person can be filled with conflict and confused and not know it because defense mechanisms may drive the painful symptoms deeper, suppressing them without addressing them constructively. When appreciation of this is precipitated, whether by deliberate attention or overwhelming of the defense mechanisms by the suppressed energy of their object, the feelings of pain and confusion are part of the realization of failed or incomplete integrity. This may be experienced in a quasi-moral sense, as cowardice or dishonesty about oneself. But even without this moral charging of the issue, one can see that the lack is a lack of integrity in the sense of the potential wholeness and integration of one's historical self-understanding. Reconstituting it needs courage, honesty, and imagination. Sometimes the effort at reconstitution may even seem almost more painful than recognition and retention of a significant self-deception or internal conflict. One may feel at least some comfort in familiarity and believe that there may be more at risk in facing up to realities. This dialectic of conflict can reach a crisis point, where what is almost a leap of conversion is required. One must decide and make an effective choice about what sort of person it is worth while to be.

We have seen how a person's conception of himself can suffer distortion by the individual's misrepresenting the past or future. Fantasy and self-deception can exact a heavy toll on self-understanding. Even the significance of the present can be misrepresented. While the present has a kind of urgency and reality the past and future do not have it still must be fitted into a life history that really does extend into both past and future, and they too have legitimate claims on us. An exaggeration of the present would involve failure to connect it with the past and or the future, to see it as somehow independent of them. The error of this is in not acknowledging the causal influence of one's past or not acknowledging foreseeable effects of one's action that are not diminished in significance by being ignored.[8] One can no more successfully live exclusively in the present than in the past or future. To try to do so is to attempt a substitution that cannot be made. While in one sense having an exclusive concern for the present seems not only reasonable but indispensable, there is also a sense in which it is a way of denying real and ineliminable dimensions of one's life. It is a way of failing or refusing to see oneself as having a history.

Earlier, in discussing character, I remarked that having reflective, critical concern for what one's motives are and for how actions affect oneself and others is part of the constructive activity of rational agency. It is a way of taking oneself and others seriously. Not to have this concern is a mark of shallowness. The same principle holds for how an individual regards his life history overall. To take into account one's life as a unified, temporally-extended whole is part of a realistic, responsible conception of it. This involves striving to understand one's past and formulating a reasonable constellation of plans, intentions, and expectations with respect to the future. One must exert oneself in both directions. What is at stake here is not just the success of one's undertakings as judged by criteria of efficiency, but also one's normative self-conception. It is rational to take care not to undertake things we are likely to feel shame or guilt about later on. And it is important not to deceive ourselves about those things in our past about which we feel guilt or shame, self-esteem, and so on. As Rawls points out:

> We should indeed be surprised if someone said that he did not care about how he will view his present actions later any more than he cares about the affairs of other people (which is not much, let us suppose). One who rejects equally the claims of his future self and the interests of others is not only irresponsible with respect to them but in regard to his own person as well. He does not see himself as one enduring individual.[9]

The unity of a life history is not like an empty container that needs to be filled in. The idea of a container, even an empty one, already lends it too much form. The unity is something constructed and achieved through

---

[8]In an excellent illustration of this sort of character, Hardy, in *Far From the Madding Crowd*, The New Wessex Edition, London, Macmillan, London, Ltd., 1974, p. 188, describes Sgt. Troy as follows:

> He was a man to whom memories were an encumbrance, and anticipations a superfluity. Simply feeling, considering and caring for what was before his eyes, he was vulnerable only in the present. His outlook upon times was as a transient flash of the eye now and then: that projection of consciousness into days gone by and to come, which makes the past a synonym for the pathetic and the future a word for circumspection, was foreign to Troy. With him the past was yesterday; the future, to-morrow; never the day after.

[9]*A Theory of Justice*, pages 422–423.

formation and presentation of materials supplied by experience, memory, intention, and expectation. There is no mold into which the materials are fitted. Depending upon what perspective one takes on oneself the materials will be weighted and shaped in various ways, some more partial or fragmented, or delusory, honest, courageous, or biased than others. An honest appraisal of oneself is the result of striving to integrate these different perspectives. This is not done by a committee-style heaping together of perspectives or giving each equal weight and authority. Rather, it is by seeing each as merely partial, as "local," so to speak, to one or another place in or standpoint toward one's life history. It is possible to produce an objective life history even of oneself, just as an objective narrative of other histories is possible. It is not easy, but it can be done. It is difficult enough to be objective about an event in which one participates.[10] The problem is not just that one's perspective is from just one place in the event and charged with one's own emotions and concerns. In addition, the actual unity of the events appears only in hindsight. One can plan a party or prepare for battle, but how it goes is often not much determined by one's plans. As John Keegan says, in discussing the Battle of Waterloo:

> It is probably otiose to point out that the "five phases" of the battle were not perceived at the time by any of the combatants, not even, despite their points of vantage and powers of direct intervention in events, by Wellington or Napoleon. The "five phases" are, of course, a narrative convenience.[11]

It is perhaps even more difficult to be objective about oneself. But there is an analogy between the participatory context and the context of one's own history in that both contexts contain no unfolding, preformed sequence. The individual (whether a self or a battle) takes shape as it develops. The disanalogy, though, and it is an important one, is that an individual person regards his or her life as a unity, while a battle is an artifact of a sort, that does not. What gives unity to a battle, even if only a very messy unity, are the various perspectives and intentions of the different persons involved.

We can strive for objectivity concerning a battle or a social event by finding out as much as we can about the subjects involved. It is not just places, dates, and numbers of people that make an account objective. That

---

[10]The Duke of Wellington referring to Waterloo once remarked:

> The history of the battle, is not unlike the history of a ball! Some individuals may recollect all the little events of which the great result is the battle lost or won; but no individual can recollect the order in which, or the exact moment at which, they occurred, which makes all the difference as to their value or importance.

I am quoting this from J. Keegan, *The Face of Battle*, Penguin Books, New York, NY, 1978, p. 117.

[11]Ibid, p. 128.

information is just data that is part of the account. If a general or a hostess has very little conception of the overall totality of events that too is part of the objective account. I have been using notions such as adequacy and accuracy so far in characterizing the properties of a well-constructed personal narrative. Think back, for example, to what it was like to find someone's diary and to read about yourself from his perspective. Recall how your reactions precipitated a new stance toward that person and toward yourself. Fitting that experience and its after-shocks into your personal narrative *now* is a quite different business than when the events and feelings were "fresh." We find similar reactions occurring when we reread old letters, even letters we ourselves have written. The fact that the story keeps undergoing change and new unities are imposed as portions of one's life are fitted together does not undo or impede objectivity with respect to oneself. Proper regard for that fact is part of it. Objectivity in this regard is not primarily conformity of thought to some independent object which is apprehended indifferently. It is honest reflection and willingness to exert oneself in confronting one's motives, acts, experiences, and emotions, and how they matter.

We can enrich our narratives with enormous amounts of detail and intricate explanatory connections but still fail to produce an account that is accurate and adequate. Rousseau's *Confessions* is perhaps a good example of this. It exhibits a certain kind of honesty, or at least openness, but the openness is crippled by paranoia and continual retreat into defensive modes of self-serving interpretation. We learn a great deal about Rousseau but it is often not what he tells us about himself but rather what is *suggested* by what he tells. There is an arabesque of self-delusion woven through his story, and the subjectivity he courageously expresses runs afoul of its own excesses. There is unity but it is an almost oppressive unity of certain overworked rationalizations.

There is no fixed set of rules or formulas to follow to achieve accuracy and adequacy in one's personal narrative. So many factors are involved and so many of them act against being objective about ourselves. But there is a real and significant difference between sound and unsound historical self-conceptions. I have claimed that one's own agency is more intelligible than other causes and dimensions in one's history. We turn now to the relation between virtue, the maximal exercise of agency, and self-understanding.

Chapter 3

Agency, Virtue, and Intelligibility

The main claims of the account so far are that a personal life history has a teleological structure and unity brought about by the individual, that the distinctive capacities of persons are teleological in a full-fledged sense, and that persons are agents who can organize and direct the operation of their capacities. By virtue of their constitution persons have the intrinsic end of self-enjoyment, but they must specify and strive to realize particular ends that give content to it.

It is also the teleology of personhood that is the source and determinant of the character of moral value. The teleology of personhood informs and connects moral phenomena. Issues of character, responsibility, motive, purpose, and so forth matter in the interrelated ways that they do because of the peculiar features of personal life histories.

I will discuss several interconnected topics in this chapter on virtue. Most of what I say concerns virtue's relation to agency, self-understanding, and self-enjoyment. But in the next couple of pages I want to say something about how the theory of persons grounds an objective conception of moral value, and why the morality it grounds is a morality of the virtues. I will not be explicating particular virtues or attempting to develop an ethic of virtue with specific content. But agency, or self-determination itself indicates much of importance with respect to what an ethic of virtue requires. The key here is the notion of respect for persons because they are self-determining. This is crucial because of how it connects to self-enjoyment. Self-enjoyment is an end that is an objective good. It is objective because it is intrinsic to the constitution of persons and it is a good because it is that toward which the exercise of person-capacities is directed. *Your* self-enjoyment is not as such a good to me. But there are decisive reasons for me to acknowledge that you should be able to pursue it. There is nothing privileged about being me or about my self-enjoyment. Respect, in the sense of concern for one's good, is owed to others, as persons, not on account of their talents, abilities, or accomplishments. It is because persons as such are self-determining beings who direct the exercise of their capacities toward an end which we recognize as intrinsically good. No individual's good has priority in and of itself over anyone else's. And the ground for the respect owed to another is non-contingent; it is located in their nature. This does not commit anyone to an affective concern for another's self-enjoyment. Nor does it legislate a logic that is only avoidable on pain of contradiction. It does give objective reasons for certain sorts of concern for and attitudes to others, and the reasons are not contingently grounded in one's circumstances or variable relations. They are based on fundamental considerations about what it is to be a person, and persons' needs and goods. Moral concern is not a matter of satisfying formal criteria of rationality, but rather guiding one's action by a certain sort of understanding. This understanding is reflected in our actions as a component of virtue. The virtues are dispositions reflecting our reasoning based upon considerations of objective goodness. Virtue is an ordering of agency to the good, and I shall argue that it conduces to one's one self-enjoyment because it is a maximal exercise of agency. Whether in fact one is moral or not is an internal, contingent matter of commitment. But the answer to the question "why should I be concerned about respecting others?" is in part, the same as the answer to the question "why should I pursue self-enjoyment?" It involves the acknowledgement of a non-contingent limit, an intrinsic good. The transfer of concern for one's good to that of another is not affected by deduction, but by volition. But the volition can be guided by good reasons accessible to anyone. They are reasons indicated by the distinctive teleology of the nature of persons, and their characteristic needs and goods. The virtues promote personal goods and are needed in order for us to live well. At the core of the notion of living well is self-enjoyment. Virtue conduces to one's own self-enjoyment and also to that of others. It is a condition we can acknowledge to involve a value to protect and promote.

    Being virtuous does not require emotional vacancy or elimination of passion and appetite. Virtue has to do with the manner of organization and translation into motive and action of our passions and appetites and so on. Even for the person who sees morality as essentially involving extension of sympathy and regards *feeling* as motivationally basic, rendering this attitude practically efficacious is a matter of rational agency. One cannot choose to have natural virtue. Rational self-determination is required to shape, orient, and execute one's moral concern. Perhaps the significance of reasons to acknowledge and be concerned for the good of others cannot catch hold unless there is at least some affective motivational base. But the development of moral awareness and virtuous character is not simply (or even primarily) a matter of extending that base. The material supplied by feeling must be informed by habits of rational self-determination, or we will be unable to appreciate the moral significance of our actions. These habits of rational self-determination constitute the well-ordering of one's own teleology and the well-ordering of our relations with each other. We will be returning to some of these points about the general outlines of a theory of moral value later on.

The central idea that I will develop in this chapter is what I call the Intelligibility Thesis: that virtuous actions are more fully intelligible than other kinds of actions to the agent who performs them, and so being virtuous conduces to constructing a followable, lucid, personal narrative. Developing this thesis requires three main tasks. First I will supply a general account of the character of virtue. Second, I will explicate why actions with this character are maximally intelligible and assimilate well into a historical self-conception. Third, special issues such as weakness of will, self-mastery, the difference between self-mastery and self-control, the opacity of vice and the unity of virtue will be addressed. Again, this is not an account of particular virtues or vices, but a highly general characterization of virtue and vice and their phenomenology. I will also say a bit about how virtue conduces to self-enjoyment.

The general account of virtue is much influenced by Aristotle and by Kant. I take it that virtue is the highest mode of self-determination and self-mastery. A person is responsible for his virtue or vice in that it is self-imposed, a product of their causality as an agent. One may, of course, be naturally kind, considerate of others, and so forth, but none of these characteristics is either necessary or sufficient for virtue. This is not because such natural dispositions are labile or unreliable; they may be quite stable and entrenched. But in so far as they are natural dispositions, they are the product of causes in the agent, but not his own causality. One is not virtuous by luck or just by finding oneself so. Natural tendencies of the type mentioned are not to be despised, nor are they void of moral worth for being natural as opposed to self-imposed. But complete virtue requires a different kind of cause, and it is that which gives it its distinctive and intrinsic value. It is not the difficulty of an act in which virtue resides. It is the character of its causality. One may act regularly and readily through the disposition to virtue and find it pleasing. The worth of the act is surely not diminished by the enjoyment it gives or the ease with which it is performed. But the disposition to virtue is knowingly and voluntarily self-imposed.

Whether a person is virtuous or not is more fully "up to" them than is the case with other dispositions. For example, someone may not be especially musically talented but through long effort and strong resolve may attain some measure of accomplishment as a musician. But it is still partially and crucially a matter of natural endowment how far one can succeed at this. Some people have a "knack," a flair, or an ability that others simply lack. This is especially evident in such things as athletics, mathematics, foreign language learning, and apparently even cooking. Virtue needs practice, as does playing the piano. And habituation, socialization, and context all have influence over it. But the achievement of virtue is not just or mainly a matter of encouraging and developing a natural characteristic. Rather, it is a matter of bringing about a characteristic, producing a quality through one's own authority. No one just "happens to be" virtuous.

It may be argued that because this account relies so heavily on self-determination and that this is a notoriously obscure or unprovable fact, the whole structure rests on philosophical quicksand. But the issue of freedom versus determinism does not, I believe, require a "foundational" or transcendental resolution. In this context, as in epistemology, foundationalism is not a requirement for objectivity or truth. In both contexts we can, as it were, swim without touching bottom. While the motive for foundationalism as a method of philosophical theorizing is often clear enough, the project immediately runs up against obstacles of its own creation. Why should any specific set of criteria be accorded a distinct, inviolable, nontransferable privilege? This question again and again has vexed and embarrassed foundationalism (as a general philosophical method). But the frustration of foundationalism (and its usually attendant requirement of necessary and sufficient conditions) does not condemn the results of analysis to relativism or diminish their objectivity.

I think this is particularly clear in the issue of explanatorily unifying person-phenomena through their connection to self-determination. A knock-down argument that proves freedom in some metaphysical or transcendental sense is not what is needed, and it is not my ambition to supply one here. It is my view that the most reasonable and illuminating approach in this case is to notice, gather, and organize facts about what is distinctive about persons and to theorize on that basis, rather than insisting that certain categorical and analytical demands be satisfied by revising or rejecting the facts. In the context of the facts of persons' actions and attitudes our understanding of them is facilitated by drawing together and acknowledging relations between them, not by looking for or inventing *other kinds of facts*. It does not seem to me helpful to look for a special kind of "fact" of freedom or "fact" of determinism. There isn't something more or something else the discovery or locating of which will illuminate the difficulties of explaining and understanding human action. What is needed is detail, clarity, and articulation of the available, familiar phenomena and considerations. It is certainly not helpful to simply recast person-phenomena in a manner suitable to the contours of a theory of something else, like computers. There is the danger here, as elsewhere, that analogy, and bad analogy, will be substituted for thought. As I have stressed repeatedly, these facts are explanatorily integrated through their connectedness to self-determination. That is, as it were the core modality of person-phenomena.

I have already remarked upon the problematic dualism of rational and mechanical causality that is a favorite target of Kant's critics. But his principle that a personal nature has the capacity for a distinctive kind of causality, entailing responsibility, and that this is essential to moral experience and moral evaluation is, I believe, true and important, even if we depart from his version of it. Without it, the responsibility for thought and action which makes the context of persons a value-laden context is dissolved. Compatibilists and determinists are typically satisfied to diminish or waive this responsibility. Like Hume, they are satisfied to make a distinction between types of efficient causes of actions. But I agree with Kant that doing so issues in a "wretched subterfuge."[1] People matter in ways other things do not, and they matter to themselves and to others because they are self-determining, purposive beings. That is what defines and distinguishes the characteristic teleology of their nature. The notion of self-determination is the connecting link that enables us to intelligibly tie together the phenomena of deliberation, decision, integrity, guilt, shame, respect, resentment, self-esteem, and other phenomena peculiar to and integral to the context of persons. And we are able to make sense of and reliably employ concepts of these phenomena even if they rarely occur in a "pure" state and are typically mixed with various circumstantial and other internal and external causal factors.

Self-determination, as I have argued, is *constructive*. The exercises of its capacities direct thought and action, shape character, and figure in the production of an account of one's history. I shall argue that moral character is more fully determined by it than by any other facts about a person. It is one thing to tie the moral dimension of personhood to self-determination. But I am also claiming that virtue is that activity over which self-determination is maximally efficacious. After traversing the steps in the argument for this we will get the result that being virtuous can contribute in an especially rich and stable way to self-enjoyment. So, there is at least that reason to be moral. Being moral promotes self-enjoyment.

In order to spell out the relation between self-determination and virtue we will contrast it to that between weakness or vice and self-determi-

[1]This remark is on p. 99 of the L. W. Beck translation of *Critique of Practical Reason*, Bobbs-Merrill, Indianapolis, IN, 1956.

nation. My claim is that weakness and vice are formally similar in that both involve forfeiture of agency but retention of responsibility. Both involve avoidable failures of agency.

It is a failure of agency because weakness and vice are determined by non-agent causes. The latter are causes in the agent and he may know them and their operation well. But the motive and character of a weak or vicious act are not a consequence of what agency imparts to them. Agency is a partner in weakness and vice in that both involve voluntariness and may also involve exertions of practical reason. But the material component of the motive and end of the act are supplied by a non-agent cause. Some of the kinds of these causes are familiar: desire, jealousy, revenge, lust, hatred, frustration, impatience, and so on. Even indifference counts among these. Viciousness need not be mean-spirited. The virtuous person is not exempt from or unsusceptible to these sorts of emotions, attitudes, and feelings. But he does not permit them to determine his acts. One may feel jealousy intensely in a painful, relentless way, but still resist the rage it can provoke or the meanness it can motivate. Part of the explanation for why we feel guilt, shame, or remorse when we act from weakness or vice is that we acknowledge that we could have done otherwise, that the act was avoidable. It is the *causality* of the act that bothers us. It is partially in the causality of the act that its wrongness, imprudence, or culpability resides.

It is because persons are able to criticize, evaluate, and exercise a measure of control over their desires, appetites, and feelings that they can exercise causality over their actions. Merely to have a desire or a feeling is not to be moved to act by it. Some desires surely are compulsive or irresistible, but these are exceptions to the norms of our capacities for action. Nor is this simply a contrast between internal and external motivation. Physical and psychological coercion and compulsion may occur in modes that are internal, external, or mixed. Free action is not simply that which occurs in the absence of external constraint. My point is that to a crucial extent the individual himself determines what shall have the force of constraint. Whether and how various potential causes are translated into action largely depends on the agent. This is true in general and not just for occasional episodes of moral significance. But it has a special importance for morality in that moral character is a reflection of self-determination.

Of course certain characteristics and propensities are reinforced by habit, example, socialization, and so forth. One may be "trained" in greed or selfishness just as one may be "trained" in moderation or consideration of others. Part of one's historical self-understanding involves reflecting upon how and why one has come to have certain dispositions, attitudes, and characteristics. A history of insecurity, deprivation, and competition for attention and satisfactions may leave a deeply entrenched influence. Examples of the force of history and context on a person's outlook, values, and attitudes toward the self and others are easily multiplied and not to be discounted. But one's history and context do not automatically supply excusing conditions for weakness or vice, nor do they alternatively make virtue inevitable. The thrust of the first two chapters was to show that persons can contribute decisively to their history, and, thus, succeed or fail to exercise authority over and responsibility for themselves.

Determining whether and to what extent weakness or vice figure in action can be difficult. For example, some people may believe that they simply "cannot bring themselves" to report some awful truth to loved ones, a truth that will be very painful and disturbing. Indeed, they may rationalize that failing to do so is not wrong, unfair, or weak, but evidence of depth of devotion and feeling. There are many plausible scenarios in which we may be inclined to excuse this sort of failing. Or, we may excuse it in that peculiar way in which we combine belief that the act is wrong, belief that it was avoidable, and make allowance for it because of its motive. I suppose love or concern not to hurt another often does reach this troubled condition, where it appears acceptable to forfeit the truth. But even here there remains the question of whose pain is the primary object of avoidance. Is it that of the reporter of the unhappy news or the recipient? I am not here making out a case for a Kantian principle of truth-telling no matter what. Rather, I am indicating what sorts of considerations figure in assessing the character of an act. My guess is that if the love is genuine, it will not be so blind as not to see the act as a wrongful, avoidable deception (supposing that telling the truth would cause pain, but not other harm). The lie will be compounded with guilt. Sometimes it is extremely difficult to tell the truth. But what interferes with it is generally not a force as great as, say, the fear one might experience in grave danger or the coercive force of realistic and drastic threats. Truth-telling contrasts with these in the respect that one's control over it (except under certain types of exceptional duress) extends right up to the making of the utterance. And the guilt or shame is often simultaneous with the lie, in the way that it is often simultaneous with a vicious remark. One gives in to a cause that can be thwarted and that one believes should be.

Isn't there a symmetry then with *succeeding* in, say, telling the truth? Why isn't this also yielding to the strength of a non-agent cause, namely, adherence to a principle? The answer is yes and no. Adherence to a principle can be pathological. When it is, we might say that the individual is exercising a certain sort of self-control, but *not* self-mastery. It is control in the respect that the adherence is deliberate and explicit. The person may be the sort who can truthfully say, "Look, I just don't tell lies". But the ground of the adherence is not in his agency. It may be grounded in rigorous indoctrination, fear of punishment, fear that the lies will flow fast and furiously if an exception is made, like a reformed alcoholic's fear of a drink, fear of loss of credibility, and so on. All of these are non-agent causes that corrupt the moral character of the principle. Perhaps in this case the pathology is benign. But it is a pathology nonetheless. Recognition of the causes of one's actions would lead either to an acknowledgement of their motivation, or to a self-deception about it: "at least I'm not a liar; that's good." But again, here the truth-telling follows weakness, not strength. It is not the agent that brings it about. Where the latter is the case, there is an asymmetry with weakness and vice.

I am not arguing that because a person does not choose her pathology she cannot choose to be weak or vicious. She can. A person can willingly and readily succumb to causes operating in her. One's vices may be such that she does not will to have it any other way. But a person cannot, on the strength of deliberation or agency, decide to be jealous, mean, selfish, or intemperate. Such motives occur in one according to causes that one does not choose to have or not. Deliberation and agency can control what becomes of those causes. So, someone may just be a jealous person or an impatient person, but still not allow her actions to be governed by jealously or impatience. But you cannot will to feel jealousy or impatience. Nor can you will to feel sympathy or compassion or consideration of others. The principle holds for "positive" pathologies too. But one can act considerately, patiently or altruistically even without affective prompting.

Aristotle regarded vice and weakness as different from each other in the respect that, for example: a self-indulgent person is led on by his own choice, since he believes that he should always pursue the pleasure of the moment. A morally weak man, on the other hand, does not think he should, but pursues it, nonetheless.[2]

Thus, the vicious character is such on account of choosing to act in conformity with a wrong rule. The weak person has the right rule in mind, but does not exercise his knowledge, translate it into action. Instead, Aristotle says, "Moral weakness does not occur in the presence of knowledge in the strict sense, and it is sensory knowledge, not science, which is dragged about by emotion."[3] The perception that judgment requires is thereby distorted and obscured.

Also, while Aristotle says that "A vicious man is not aware of his vice, but a morally weak man knows his weakness,"[4] he does believe that the vicious man is responsible for his vice and that virtue and vice are both voluntary. Along the lines of the present account we can make a similar claim in that the vicious person elevates wrong rules and criteria to a level of stable acceptability. Vice is voluntary but it tends to chronically and extensively obscure and impede the right operation of agency. Because of this the vicious man may be unaware of his vice, as vice. But viciousness is not primarily ignorance or the result of ignorance. It is more of the nature

[2]Aristotle's *Nicomachean Ethics*, trans. M. Ostwald, Bobbs-Merrill, Indianapolis, IN, 1146b 22 25.

[3]Ibid, 1147b 15–16.

[4]Ibid, 1150b 35.

of error or failure than ignorance or lack. The vicious individual is capable of knowledge but fails to employ it in deliberation, choice, and action. This can *lead to* systematically poor perception and bad judgment and thus reinforce its own erroneousness. Viciousness *feels* different from weakness and may not even pay the price of regret, but it shares with weakness a general form, a failure of rational agency.

The main question here is "why should agency as a cause yield morally right, non-akratic action?" I want to say a bit about Kant's answer to this question not because I think it is an altogether right answer, but because it is an important and instructive one. His account of the criteria for the moral worth of an action is formalistic and legalistic in a way that my own is not. His answer to this question is that agency is *rational* causality in a peculiar sense. It is not just distinct from non-agent causality, but in its very character as causality *in accordance with the concept of law* contains and constitutes the moral validity of actions. Law-likeness, in Kant's account involves necessity and universality. Actions satisfying the conditions of the law of freedom, the Categorical Imperative, are unconditioned by any causality that could diminish their moral worth. Or, to put it differently, actions determined by a law of freedom are ipso facto objectively morally necessary and unadulterated by subjective, contingent, empirical determinants. Kant was concerned to preserve a distinction between the worth of persons and that of non-persons, and correlatively, preserve and explicate the distinct character of moral motivation. Because persons are self-determining a special attitude is owed to them, an attitude of respect. Principles of action that do not satisfy the criteria of necessity and universality of the Categorical Imperative (Kant thought) involve either precarious judgments of the good or have a (more or less disguised) selfish character. The form of practical reason alone comprehends the personhood of all. Even "what's in it for *us*, all of us?" is no better a criterion than "what's in it for me?" when compared to "what is owed to anyone?" It is only acting through rational agency as a cause that the respect owed to persons as self-determining beings can be secured. This of course includes oneself as well as others. An attitude of respect is owed to persons because of the formal character of the causality they are capable of.

The Kantian "package" as a whole is enormously difficult, obscure, and problematic. My own account is not offered as a version of it. I do not base moral concern for oneself or others on the formal conditions of law-likeness. But I do believe our causality is a necessary means to our objective good, and so rational agency is central to the groundwork of morality. Since this is true for any person there is a reason to respect persons. Again, I do not mean that because there is an objective good for persons there is a reason which is sufficient to motivate moral attitudes and dealings. I am sure that one could understand that there is a good for persons and yet be profoundly immoral. A reason, even a very strong one, does not of itself motivate. To be motivationally efficacious one must want to act for it. That is, whether one is moral or not is an internal matter of commitment that is contingent, *even though* there is a decisive reason to be moral.

Acting in a morally worthy manner involves maximal exercise of one's causality. In this respect, I think the Kantian notion is sound, though I do not accept his explanation of it. Agency is not maximized through elimination of content in striving to satisfy a formal ideal of rationality. Agency has a telos, self-enjoyment. This telos is not realizable through the operation of causes other than rational self-determination. It need not (and indeed cannot) be altogether unmixed with other causes. But they are not adequate to it. Non-agent causes are at best only contingently connected to the realization of the teleology of persons. They operate independently of what the individual imparts to them.

But we can make out the relation of agency to virtue without being driven into the noumenal world. I believe we can best understand virtues as powers ordered in certain ways. A person has different types of powers or capacities, among them the physiological and sensitive ones characteristic of their biological species, and rational powers. Acting virtuously involves a certain sort of rational ordering of a power, in a manner that is habitual. It is on the basis of how one's powers are ordered that they have certain morally relevant characteristics. The agency involved in acquiring and exercising virtue is a matter of rationally directed and regulated exertion. Agency is power with a rational teleology, but this does not entail that its standard is purely formal. Normative considerations about the operation of practical reason have to do with the extent to which a person acts for reasons and what those reasons are. Agency is a power that one directs, rather than a power that operates through mechanisms a person does not control. We can be moved by powers of appetite and affect. And we can be moved by powers of self-determination, freeing ourselves thereby from causes operating in or on us. My claim is that the morally significant character of actions and dispositions turns on the extent to which it is shaped by rational self-determination.

Thus, my answer to the question "why should agency as a cause yield morally right, non-akratic action?" is that agency has a distinctive relation to the objective good for persons. It is the cause of it. This does not entail that I will be concerned for your self-enjoyment just as in being concerned for my own. But it does give me a reason, and an objective one, for being concerned for your self-enjoyment. I have to choose to accept it, make it a motivationally efficacious reason. But its being a reason is not grounded in any subjective or contingent facts about me or anyone else. It is a reason grounded in the nature of agency. To be morally concerned for persons, to have moral concern for them (including oneself) involves exercising rational causality. It involves acting in a manner such that the principle of action is informed by the conception of what is good for them as persons.

This cannot be supplied by non-agent causes. To maximize agency is not to act from respect for the abstract laws of a kingdom of abstract ends. It is to commit oneself to realizing a real and contentful end which each person has by virtue of being a person, i.e. self-enjoyment. It is to regulate one's constructive rationality by an understanding of the nature of persons.

Agency is a rationally regulated and guided power in a way that other powers are not. Or, rather, agency is the power to act in a rationally regulated way, the power to construct and pursue ends on the basis of understanding, judgment and evaluation. Of course what is good for oneself and others involves considerations about contingent and subjective matters of need, desire, and feeling. Part of showing concern for others is respecting their feelings, trying to understand them and not just seeing the situation as a bloodless, abstract instance of a moral law. Judgments of what is good and appropriate are often subtly nuanced and carefully calibrated to personalities and circumstances. Virtue needs to be adaptable and discriminating. But the basic contours of both characteristic human goods and the morally virtuous manner of realizing them are grounded in the nature of agency as a power of rational self-determination. If there are general or universal principles of morally right action they are principles generated from considerations about what conduces to self-enjoyment. And acting in a manner that answers to this involves maximally exercising one's agency, involves virtue. It is not a mystery or a lucky coincidence that the same causality that maximizes one's own self-enjoyment is an essential element of moral action. It is a right ordering of the power for rational action, of self-determination, guided by a conception of what is good, that is not merely consequent upon subjective, private, or contingent phenomena.

The main component of self-enjoyment, that component that yields the richest and most stable enjoyment, is being a self-determining being. Pleasure, Aristotle says, completes the activity of a perfect or unimpeded capacity or organ.[5] When a capacity or organ is functioning well, pleasure is involved in the activity, the pleasure being that which is proper to its organ or capacity. In this account, self-enjoyment is a distinct type of pleasure consequent upon the well-functioning of one's practical rationality. Its formal cause is the exercise of one's capacity for action governed by reason. It is that which is essentially desirable for its own sake and worthwhile. It is because this is so that persons have a reason to strive to realize self-conceptions and achieve self-enjoyment. The operation of non-agent causes can be pleasing, and a person may experience those pleasures without ever achieving self-enjoyment. But the self-determination involved in the pursuit of self-enjoyment lends it a distinct and superior character of pleasure. It is *oneself* that one enjoys, not just something happening to or in oneself.

---

[5]The treatment of pleasure that I am basing these claims on is in Book X, Chapter 5 of the *Nicomachean Ethics*.

I have argued that the character of virtue resides in its causality and that agency determines this character. It is for this reason that whether or not people are virtuous is a matter under their own authority and responsibility. Moreover, being virtuous contributes in a special way to self-enjoyment. This does not render virtue self-interested, since it is not a contingent, subjective interest of the self that is being promoted. I want to be clear about distinguishing this view from certain versions of egoism.

We need to understand two different senses of egoism. According to the first, oneself and one's interests are privileged. The value of one's ends and activities turns on how effectively they maximize one's interests in an *exclusive* sense. This is generally regarded as a poor if possible morality, making for highly adversarial and precarious relations between people. Egoism of this sort, if not crude, is selfish. But there is another sense of egoism according to which being moral conduces to one's own good, but both what being moral is, and the reason to be moral are *not* explicated in the exclusive sense of self-interest. In this broader sense, even Kant is an egoist in that acting freely and maintaining justified self-respect are especially prized. Being moral is a good for the individual, but it is not a good that one pursues through competitive, selfish practices. The reasons for activities being morally justified do not refer exclusively to private interest. To act morally is to take into account (practically not just affectively) what promotes the good for people, and to undertake to do it because that is what it is. That is, the rationality that apprehends the facts and circumstances is action-guiding as rational agency. In being moral one does what is good, and it is a good for oneself to do so because of how agency is related to self-enjoyment.

There are people who deliberately cultivate habits of selfishness and disregard the interests and welfare of others. Some even seem to enjoy this a good deal and take pleasure in frustrating, humiliating, or denying others. They may even regard their meanness as a kind of strength, a way of controlling and frightening others. But whether one is just self-interested or also malicious about it, egoism is particularly inapt to conduce to self-enjoyment. While the egoist (who is not just someone pushed and pulled by impulse and appetite and emotion) has a general conception of conforming action to certain sorts of reasons, he is moved and guided by what Kant called pathology. He mistakes *his* having an interest or desire with there being a justificatory reason, a morally validating reason to act accordingly. Instead of striving to conform his motivations to reasons, he mistakes the latter for the former. The egoist mistakes the virtues as impediments to pursuing his good, and to the extent that he succeeds at being an egoist, he forfeits his agency, and aggrandizes his pathology. The virtues are not inhibitors of self-enjoyment. They are the most reliable, effective means to it. They partially constitute one's good, and like Aristotle I believe that the virtues are something good in themselves. As Aristotle says, we would choose them, "even if no further advantage would accrue from them—but we also choose them partly for the sake of happiness, because we assume that it is through them that we will be happy."[6] It is my view that self-enjoyment and being virtuous coincide in being consequent upon the activity of rational agency.

To summarize the claims thus far: there are reasons to be moral, grounded in objective considerations about personal goods; being moral essentially involves rational self-determination, that is, virtue; and virtue contributes crucially to self-enjoyment because it is a maximal exercise of rational self-determination.

We will address more fully the relation between virtue and self-enjoyment and also self-knowledge later on. Here I want to return to the thesis that weakness and vice both involve failure of agency.

The fact that in akratic or vicious action the individual does not determine the cause does not imply that its cause and character will be surprising, alien, or confusing to the person who performs it. He may know a good deal about the influences he is susceptible to and how it feels to be subject to them. For example, someone who is recovering from an ulcer may deliberately avoid taking alcoholic drinks even though he enjoys them because he knows they will aggravate his condition and cause him pain. He may generally have little difficulty staying with his therapeutic regimen. But suppose on a certain occasion this person indulges in a few celebratory drinks, say, in some sort of private little ritual with friends he has not seen for a long while. The rationalizations may flow easily, with the ulcer patient disbelieving them even as he utters them. In a case such as this the causality of the behavior is surely not puzzling or mysterious. When one asks "what made me do it?" in a situation like this, it is typically not a genuine inquiry about the cause or character of the act. It is a way of expressing the question "why did I allow myself to do it?" This may have as presuppositions: "I knew I shouldn't" or "I wish I hadn't". We often do things we both believe we shouldn't do and acknowledge to be avoidable. This does not free us from responsibility and it is just because of this that we feel guilt or self-reproach. These performances are *lapses* from what we regard as standards of conduct that are completely attainable.

Not all weakness of will is morally wrongful, nor is it all dispositional. It may be morally indifferent, occasional, and episodic. But acts of vice and the disposition to moral viciousness both involve forfeiture of agency, as does weakness, though the latter may be disguised by a benign pathology.

A weak person's dispositions may regularly coincide with what virtue would have them do, but they are not a substitute for it. Even feelings of

[6]Ibid, 1097b 1–5.

kindness, tolerance, and sympathy may be morally misapplied and do not of their own impart virtue to the actions they motivate. These sorts of motives do figure in our willingness to excuse agents and are used to explain away culpability or blame. We are more likely to excuse the charitable or sensitive person than the individual whose virtue is tarnished by priggishness or officiousness, or the individual who is just plain reckless, selfish, or dishonest. How many times do our moral judgments run up against sincere sentiments such as "I was trying to give him a break," or "how would you feel?" and so forth? But misdirected warmth is a failure of agency as is mean-spiritedness. So-called "natural virtue" is not to be inhibited or denigrated. But the sentiments and dispositions that constitute it need to be directed by reasons and judgments which they cannot supply. I am not advocating emotional barrenness as a condition of virtue or a component of moral strength. Self-mastery is not just a matter of denial or indifference to passions, feelings, and emotions. But a contribution from the side of agency is required in order that they do not fail to redeem their moral value or have only cosmetic effect. The virtuous individual need not have any less strong feelings than anyone else. But he exercises power over how their influence figures in his thought and action.

Weakness can become entrenched and lead to viciousness when the person permits a cause to operate regularly. This may involve rationalization in the following way. An individual may, for example, give in to or be overcome by jealous impulses, "a jealously so strong that judgment cannot cure," in Iago's words. The motive and opportunity for this may occur with some frequency. Eventually, he just comes to regard himself as a jealous person, not only in the respect of having the feelings, but also of acting on them. His explanation will be "look, that's the sort of person I am," as though susceptibility to performing certain kinds of acts were no more voluntary than susceptibility to indigestion from eating certain foods. Even if one does not want to be that sort of person, the idea that one is can become entrenched in his conception of himself, and thus make it more likely that he really *will* come to be like that. Here is a case where, to an extent, thinking it can make it so. Certain matters of temperament which, as habits of mind and affect, are amenable to control may themselves become controlling, though the individual is still responsible for his responses and actions.

It is because one's responsibility figures centrally in a process of this sort that the development of the given characteristic is intelligible to the individual. He may come to feel remorse or anger at himself for having "let himself go," much as weight gain or types of intemperance lead to similar responses. There is no guarantee that the person will feel angry at himself or make an effort to overcome the weakness in which he has indulged. He may find it easier not to reflect upon and criticize himself. He also may do those things but continue to be weak and compound it with self-deception.

But for many action-dispositions the explanation "that's just the way I am" is simply false, just as "I couldn't help it" is simply false for many action explanations.

I remarked earlier that sometimes upon reflection, weakness and even vice are intelligible to the agent insofar as he sees that it is his own failure of agency that underlies it. He may admit that a self-deception or rationalization was a party to the action, and see through it. But in many cases this level of clarity is not attained. Either the agent is insufficiently reflective and fails to reach an understanding of his actions, or in spite of a reflective, self-critical standpoint they remain confusing and opaque. I do not mean this in the sense that the individual does not know just what he has done, but that he cannot fully understand why he did it. This is especially disturbing if the actions or dispositions are of a kind that the person wishes he were free of susceptibility to. For example, someone may constantly pursue diversions from an undertaking that is important to him. He may just find that he can't get on with his work. He is committed to the project, wants to follow through with it, and even feels that his self-esteem is bound-up with doing so. But there are always enough reasons and excuses to "put it off," do other things, and render the project's completion less likely even as it becomes more crucial. Shopping, cleaning, drinking, reading detective novels, or whatever may replace getting to work and become practically neurotic behaviors. The more one diverts oneself the more pressing and obsessional the need to get on with the task becomes. "Why don't I just sit down and do it?" "Why can't I discipline myself?" and like questions constantly agitate. Perhaps it is a lack of confidence, a fear of failure, or some other natural and real enough worry that seems to be the main obstacle. The individual may acknowledge this and also believe that he has the capability to overcome it and yet continue to fail to do so. So there is a story he can tell about himself, but in a way the story reports or describes his situation without adequately explaining it. The symptoms are well known, the path to health understood; he just doesn't understand what is incapacitating him. It is not enough to diagnose his condition as weakness. He already knows he's being weak. This is an example of what I mean by weakness involving an etiology which is opaque relative to agency. Even if a particular past episode can be identified which has led to fear anxiety, or another undermining cause, the understanding that that is the case still will not render the etiology of the failure transparent. After all, how often do we understand the obstacle but not why we do not overcome it? I may know what the cause is but not why I yield to it.

Similarly with the phenomenon of moral corruption. Suppose that out of anger at someone who has lied to me in a way that is very hurtful I do something I have never done before. I lie to them. I have always been honest with them and to others, but the painful episode is so effective at making me vengeful that I go ahead and lie. I lie to them again and then again and gradually find that while lying is still pretty distasteful to me, I can do it with the same facility as telling the truth. In fact, I become good at it. I find that it may make me a bit uneasy but that it sometimes seems to have the atrractions of sport. While I believe that I can "turn it on and off" I find that turning it on is now almost effortless. I begin to wonder about this new near-habit of mine, and truth-telling starts to involve a bit more exertion. I find that lying is easy but being a liar is not. I don't like being a liar. But I don't understand very well why I do it though the initial motive is not in doubt. I do understand that it was a powerful but not a good motive and that the proliferation of its effect was undesirable, wrong, and avoidable. I feel that the scale and ease of my dishonesty is far out of proportion with the original motive; indeed, that any dishonesty would be. Now it is not at all clear to me why I lie. And once over the pain that spurred it I am disgusted at ever having started. I can and do separate the motive from the lying. Nothing about my dishonesty was inevitable. I feel that my character is suffering corruption through these transactions and also to that extent I do not understand myself. Someone else may simply state "I lie because . . ." and fill in the blank with any of a number of unpuzzling explanations. This is not evidence that they understand themselves better than I understand myself. More likely, it is evidence that they are satisfied with a lesser self-understanding. It is easy to regard modes of corruption as natural, part of one's make-up.

What about the individual who exhibits vice in a deliberate, calculating way? Suppose he is selfish, treacherous, mean, and dishonest, and that he goes in for all of this with a sort of relish for it, delighting in his acts and their consequences. Isn't he capable of a clear self-understanding? If he believes that he is capable of it is he mistaken or deceived? It is false to simply assert that no one likes or wants to be vicious. He may even carefully choose his vices from among an extensive repertoire of possibilities.

Being vicious does not preclude acting for reasons, careful deliberation, knowing one's motives, and enjoying one's acts. But it does involve the disordering of the intrinsic teleology of person-capacities by non-agent causes. A habit of moral vice can be enjoyed as regularly and guiltlessly as smoking. What's not to understand about it? As I indicated earlier, any vice has its causes extrinsic to one's agency. And for the vicious individual his character is, in so far as it is vicious, a construct and constellation of causes not of his own making. His contribution is to select them and give them effect, to render them operational. But the etiology or moral vice essentially involves elements that are not products of agent-causality. As such they are not immediately and fully present to the understanding. They may be fully present to consciousness, but they are not on that account as intelligible as agency. The vicious person's historical self-understanding may be detailed, and integrated. But it will be a construction out of materials that obstruct the measure of intelligibility available to the virtuous individual. In virtuous activity the self as agent just is the cause; the awareness of the character of the cause coincides with its operation.

Why is historical self-knowledge important to people? I argued earlier that it facilitates effective self-determination. It illuminates and illustrates one's capacities and abilities to oneself and supplies a context, both informative and normatives for judgment and decision making. The unity, wholeness, and coherence of one's conception of his or her life are functions of the explanatory integration of the past, present, and future. More than just awareness of the past and consideration of future prospects are required for this sort of integrity. An appreciation of how they figure and fit is needed; an appreciation of explanatory relations to other components of one's history. A familiar phenomenon is awareness of some bit of the past, perhaps a painful awareness, but without successful assimilation and integration into historical self-conceptualization. The episode or feeling "stands out" and continues to attract attention, but its significance has not been determined; its relations to other feelings, decisions, and judgements are not appreciated and understood. It leaves one with a kind of phenomenological indigestion and unclear attitude.

There is no guarantee that even a combination of effort and good faith will produce a single, unified, satisfactory personal narrative. In the first place, there may be more or less reconstruction and revision. As the story goes on, attitudes toward and judgments about the past and future change. In itself this need not cause conflict or confusion, but it may. It may also lead to a more satisfactory self-understanding. But reconstruction and revision may take place on a much greater scale, and without a solid base. Ways of worldmaking, so to speak, can easily be multiplied and people may see their life histories thematically unified in a number of different and incompatible ways. Lacking genuine, stable attachment to any of these they may experience a sort of detachment from themselves, even in the present, and have no confidence about how their activity fits into a unified life. This will likely detach them from any single, guiding conception of the future as well, since they are not sure which history extends into it. This disorients and disrupts their teleology as they cannot see how their actions and choices fit into a purposive plan of life. In this situation there is no representation of one's history to adhere to which supplies a basis for imaginative departure or a background of presupposition, normative criteria, and explanatory connections. Suppose I cannot tell what overall representation of myself to conform to. This may not be disabling. It may have just the opposite effect and motivate me to a high pitch of activity, trying this, now that, frequently changing my mind and so forth. But all the while I am unable to dedicate myself with any constancy or momentum to a plan or even orientation. I may do a lot of things, but without any conviction about their importance and perhaps as a technique of avoiding my confusion. Remaining active is not the problem. Rather, it is remaining purposive in any sustained, effective way that eludes me. I become, in a way, a relativist about my life history and myself, unattached to any stable categories of self-understanding. I very much desire to be so attached but my confusion involves a fear of commitment to any such categories, as though they would induce confinement but not direction. This sort of confusion and lack of sustained purposiveness may be overcome by successes at certain undertakings, the care and encouragement of friends, and sometimes a courageous effort of will. Alternatively, it may breed further disorientation, self-doubt, and loss of self-esteem, familiarly accompanied by dramatic mood swings between optimism and despair, confidence and insecurity. One sees that happiness seems a distant, almost unapproachable goal and may even lose the ability to experience enjoyment in things. This is because there is no stable machinery employed for achieving happiness and no array of normative commitments with which to evaluate one's activities. Describing a condition of this type should indicate how important a sense of unity and structure in one's self-understanding typically is. This does not require adherence to a single plan of life or commitment to a dominant end or single motivational self-conception. But without unity, diversity and change approximate to internal discord and confusion. They become substitutes for unity rather than materials out of which it is constructed.

Also sometimes a person is characterized by a salient trait such as vanity, generosity, or ambition rather than by the ends ingredient in their self-conceptions. When asked to describe someone we might say "he's one of the most self-assured people I've ever met" rather than "he's the most successful young lawyer in this part of the state," though both are true. It depends on the person, our mood and attitude toward him, and by whom and why the question is being asked. There is rarely a single, outstanding, dominant feature of a person that obviously and adequately indicates his or her character. This is so even for a Napoleon, Elizabeth I, Goethe, or Stalin, though sometimes such individuals are known chiefly for one or two salient qualities or achievements. And an individual may not regularly think of or describe herself in terms of a dominant, pronounced, or thematic trait or end. But even if the weight and prominence of ends, commitments, attitudes, and characteristics shift and undergo changes in our historical self-understanding people can appreciate their life histories as single, unified, followable wholes. It need not and typically does not appear as a collection of distinct stories. There is no fixed pattern that unfolds in any inevitable way, but pattern and unity can be constructed, even out of diverse and changing constituents.

I have argued that persons achieve self-enjoyment through engaging in activities desired for their own sake and judged to be worthwhile. I have also argued that historical self-knowledge facilitates self-enjoyment. It is a constitutive means to it. Historical self-knowledge aids the pursuit of self-enjoyment not only by making deliberation and action more effective but also because it is desirable for its own sake. In general, given the distinctive teleology of personhood, people desire self-knowledge for its own sake and judge it to be worthwhile. Self-knowledge is a good.

I suggested earlier that what is primarily enjoyed in self-enjoyment is being a purposive being. A well-ordered teleology in a rational, deliberative being is pleasing. And self-enjoyment is realized through the effective exercise of a rational, purposive agent's capacities for thought and action. A personal narrative is a construction, a result of purposive activity, no less than striving to realize motivational self-conceptions is. It is not just a representation that occurs to one. It is a type of self-conception that incorporates both a past now closed to possibility and a future which is yet to be determined. In the respect that the past to which one is heir cannot be changed (though the interpretation and appreciation of it can be) this type of self-conception includes components different in kind from a motivational self-conception. But it is similar to the latter in that it projects into the future and is a teleologically informed construction. It is (at least potentially) both explanatory and normative. It is explanatory in its narrative unification of past and present, and normative in its connecting these to an end-oriented future. The extent to which it possesses these dimensions is person-dependent, and variable over time in any one person's life. In a mood of depression both past and future can sink like desert sand into a dry well and engagement with them be lost. But a change in attitude can restore interest in one's narrative self-understanding and reenergize it and its significance.

The claim that self-knowledge is something desirable does not imply that if I have self-knowledge I will, to that extent, like myself, be pleased, or self-satified. Also, even people with a poor self-understanding can like themselves and enjoy being who they are. This may involve suppressing certain aspects of one's character and history, but it need not. A person can do well at understanding himself and human nature but still be pessimistic about both or find them wanting in serious ways. They may fail to measure up to an ideal, or the person may be cynical or suspicious of their nature. But in general, and for the most part, self-knowledge does conduce to self-enjoyment. I may not love what I know about myself but still desire and value the knowledge. What I know about myself may indicate that I have certain limitations or that the quality of certain of my motives or desires is below standards I want to live up to. But it is still a good to me to know these things, insofar as doing so better enables me to come to terms with them rather than being a victim of them.

The virtuous individual is best able to achieve self-knowledge and derive enjoyment from it. He is best able to achieve it because his history is most fully determined by his own causality. It is the self in its practical employment that is the object of knowledge and, in the case of virtue, the self is the cause of what it understands. No one's life history is exclusively a history of virtue, but a virtuous life is maximally constructed out of the activity of self-determination. The agency of a rational nature is intelligible to the extent that it is employed. This is because to understand the exercise of agency one need not trace the etiology and diagnose the character of the motives by which one is moved to act. The etiology and responsibility of the action do not extend beyond the power of the agent to determine his action in a rationally justified manner, as they do when action involves other types of causality.

It is a consequence of these facts that being moral frees one from internal conflict, though *striving* to be moral may involve internal conflict. The virtuous individual may have to struggle against impulses, appetites, interests, and emotions.[7] But success at virtue has as a concomitant the enjoyment of one's power as a cause and also self-mastery. Mere control is an exercise of force against other forces. Mastery is a resolution of this conflict in favor of virtue. And it is this kind of unimpeded activity of a person which can contribute to self-enjoyment in a distinctively rich and stable way. It is not just the satisfaction of having done the right thing. It is the steady enjoyment of the operation of one's capacities ordered in a maximally self-governing way.

The virtuous individual's self-enjoyment will be constitutive rather than circumstantial. It is not dependent on causes and conditions not under their control. This does not condemn the weak or immoral person to a life of misery or ensure happiness to the virtuous. Nothing in the world does either of those in a completely reliable way. But the modality of virtue-generated self-enjoyment is both more secure and more complete in its effect than that of any other type. It is the result of the internal working of the teleology of persons and not just a condition accidentally in conformity with it. There is also a reason to continue to strive to realize it. Virtue-generated self-enjoyment reinforces itself. It is not a condition one grows bored with or tired of. A person can grow tired of self-control but not of self-mastery. Self-control involves a fatiguing effort to order and inhibit desires and passions. This can result in an enormous amount of tension and can make one volatile or inclined to occasional but excessive losses of control. One then feels pressure and conflict. But to the extent that a

---

[7]At 1152a 1–5 Aristotle distinguishes moral strength from tenacity:

> For being tenacious consists in offering resistance, while moral strength consists in mastering.

He also describes the self-controlled individual as different from the morally strong in that

> While a morally strong man has base appetites, a self-controlled man does not and is, moreover, a person who finds no pleasure in anything that violates the dictates of reason. A morally strong man, on the other hand, does find pleasure in such things, but he is not driven by them. 1150a 33 4.

I am using the label "self-control" differently from Aristotle, but apart from the terminological differences, my account borrows much from his.

person achieves self-mastery, the tension, conflict, and pressure are diminished. A disposition to virtue is distinct from an ability to harness akratic or vicious tendencies. One has to practice self-control in cultivating virtue but it is not the same thing as it. It differs both formally and phenomenologically. A break-down in self-control is often very pleasing, even if it meets with guilt or shame later on. It can be felt as a release or reward. This is not the case for a failure of virtue. In a failure of virtue there is no pleasure. I do not mean in any failure of a person to be virtuous, but in a virtuous person's failing. The cost, in terms of guilt or self-reproach, is not balanced against pleasure from the act, and there is no room for rationalization. What for weak or vicious individuals may be enjoyable is for virtuous individuals a corruption of integrity. This is because of how it contrasts with their general dispositions to act and their guiding understanding of themselves. For the weak person who is trying to exercise self-control the indulgence may actually conform to his self-understanding more fully than the effort at control. He may, through that effort, be trying to change his self-conception, but not yet have effected the change. For the virtuous person, a failure of virtue stands out sharply in discrepancy with his self-conception.

Virtue is never completely realized because self-mastery is never completely realized. There is no specific state or episode of completion for either. Just as health and organic teleology are always liable to defect and disorder, so is rational teleology. Neither is ever in a state of perfection. As Aristotle said of happiness, virtue and self-mastery are characteristics of a life, not of bits or portions of one. A weak or vicious person can perform virtuous acts and a virtuous person can be weak or vicious. But in each case the performances are exceptional, departures from generally guiding dispositions. It is the overall character of the dispositions as relatively stable guides of thought and action that determines virtue and self-mastery.

It is not part of this account that in order to be virtuous or achieve self-understanding one must have a special "moral" view of life and the world, that virtue is a consuming, altogether dominant end. Indeed, it is not an end in just the way that other motivational self-conceptions are. It is a manner of thought and action through which one pursues ends and engages in activities. A person can have a fundamentally aesthetic, religious, or scientific view of the world and be virtuous or not. Being virtuous primarily involves dispositions to act for certain sorts of reasons. Virtues of fairness, courage, honesty, fidelity, and so forth are not attached exclusively to particular activities and contexts and unattached to others. To strive to be virtuous is to strive to live one's life in a certain manner, in accordance with rational self-determination, and not primarily to perform this or that action.

The non-virtuous person can of course attain a measure of unity and followability but not the depth of understanding accessible to the virtuous person. For the non-virtuous person the content of his life history is not obscured, but the explanation of it is because the explanatory relations are not a reflection of causal relations of the person's own making. There may even be an overall theme, such as selfishly and ruthlessly pursued ambition. But that is not a unifying theme the individual has made through exercise of rational agency. It is a motivating principle that he allows to operate, and he may impart to it additional dimensions of rationalization, self-deception, or hypocrisy. The virtuous individual has no need to distort or rationalize his historical self-conception. His conscience will not be offended and his self-esteem not threatened. There certainly are vicious characters who are so completely morally disordered that their own history of viciousness is not an offense or threat to them. They may exhibit almost psychopathological moral indifference or outright delight in their personal record. This person accepts responsibility for himself at least in the sense that he is satisfied with his character, does not rationalize its defects, and willingly pursues his immoral ends. He is even satisfied with his historical self-conception, and is shameless and remorseless. This does not make him guiltless; it is just that he does not see himself as blameworthy and is not bothered by conscience or the results of self-examination. This agent is not a victim of weakness. He "goes in" for vice on the grounds of choice and without feeling conflict with what virtue requires of him. He likes his character. Because his life-history does not exhibit internal conflict, but instead a consistent and satisfying pattern of vicious thought and action he should seemingly have no special difficulty in achieving an explanatory, coherent historical self-understanding.

It is true that his history will not be a mystery to him or somehow inaccessible. It is not retrieval or reconstruction of the past that is problematic. Rather it is explanatory penetration that is impeded. It is one thing to record and represent to oneself the events of the past in a correct order. This is possible for anyone who is not mentally deficient or somehow incapacitated. But to do this does not represent an achievement of self-knowledge. It is awareness or apprehension without understanding. The latter involves explanatoriness, and this is something that must be brought about through an effort of reflection and judgment. But the less one's history is a history of his agency, the more difficult is the task of explanation.

The force of influences of past experiences can be obscured by time and changes in attitude toward them and by altered patterns of rationalization. Fear of recollection or guilt can suppress or disfigure past experiences. How one wants to see the past may conflict with what memory presents from it. Even where memory is accurate it may bring forward the unclarity and confusion of past experiences. Again, the opacity is not primarily in the representation of the past, but in the understanding of it. For example, in remembering making a deceitful promise, one may recall vividly the feelings present in the episode and the swarm of thoughts that occurred. But one can often remember *that* they felt or thought such-and-such but still not have a clear idea of just why they did what they did. An explanation for the false promise may be offered, such as, "I knew I couldn't be there when I said I would be, but he would have been furious if he knew the reason." It is easy to suppose that the individual was protecting himself from the fall-out of another's anger. "He would never have forgiven me, and besides, my not showing up was really no tragedy." It may seem precious or trite to ask *why* someone makes false promises in this defensive way. People do it all the time to avoid inconvenience or another's anger and for any number of other reasons. These are familiar enough sorts of explanations where it is simply a matter of one consideration outweighing another. But attaching weight to considerations is something we *do*. We partially determine how considerations figure in thought and action. The question of how these considerations get their weight and interact in producing action must also be addressed. It is in answering this question with respect to instances of weakness of will or vice that there will be unclarity. This is because *if* the agent can distinguish between what would have been the morally right thing to do and what he did he will see that what he did was avoidable *and* not based on good reasons. His action will not be adequately rationalized. What moved him may be plain enough. But that he should be so moved, that he yields to this or that impulse, emotion, or consideration will be left without a satisfactory rational justification.

Suppose someone is a clever, deliberate liar. He likes spreading false rumors, misleading others, and distracting and disrupting others in his credible but malicious way. Suppose he explains that it is good sport for him and a way to feel that he has some power, and he is amused by the tangles he leads others into. He may never bother himself with seriously addressing the question of why he lies so much and likes it so well. But suppose someone else puts the question to him and puts it in such a way that he cannot just answer it with another simple lie, such as, "I'm not dishonest. How did this story get started?" Let us suppose further that he does not at this point go in for a face-saving self-deception and lie to himself. He acknowledges the fault and begins to really think about it. He might think, "I don't know. It's just a bad habit, almost like an addiction. Some people smoke, some people cheat on their income taxes, I tell lies." But finding company for a fault is not finding an explanation of it. He understands that lying is both wrong and disreputable. Unless there is some compelling reason why he "can't help it" the explanation is that he does not exert himself to. It is a failure of will. Even if there is a story about his growing up in a distrustful household or his having been hurt by someone else's lies in the past or whatever, the account of his lying remains essentially an "internal" matter. This is not just because everybody knows lying is wrong, or that experience and circumstances, including the character and habits of others, count for nothing. It is because the wrongness of his lying is something he understands and, in the absence of extraordinary factors, it is something it is in his power to deal with. Lying may be so regular and pronounced a feature of his character that he can hardly see himself giving it up. To do so would be a painful and difficult change. But that does not explain or excuse failure at reform, especially because he can understand that there are good reasons for telling the truth. In the end, his habit of lying is to an extent unintelligible, because irrational. Not that there isn't an account of it in general and some small story for each lie. But both the general and particular accounts indicate that in his lying he does not have mastery of himself, and the contribution of his agency is equivocal and confused.

This is quite different from the situation of the compulsive or mentally disordered individual. In those cases there are causal stories that explain why they *could not* have exercised their agency. But even if normal individuals are routinely weak or morally vicious, their patterns of action are the result of a forfeiture and not an overwhelming of rational agency. Moral activity as a function of constructive, deliberative rationality is still possible for them. The life history of the virtuous person is a construction of motives, purposes, and actions achieved through the exercise of rational authority over himself. To be virtuous is to direct one's life in a manner wherein self-determination is maximally exercised across the various dimensions of activity, engagement, and interaction. It includes temperance, civility, and honesty as well as altruism and fairness. It is because of how agency figures in this that the virtuous person's life history is intelligible to him.

While I have spoken of the relation of virtue to the unity of a person's life history I have not addressed the issue of the unity of the virtues. But there is an important relation between these two unities. Moral virtue requires agency. Agency is a power of rational self-determination, a power to act under the guidance of reasons and evaluations. The dispositions that constitute the various virtues are not isolated from each other. They are various orderings of our powers of agency. They *are* unified in that their presence and their operation are never completely autonomous with respect to the other. They are not distinct from each other in the way that say, being quick-witted and having a good memory are. It is not just that the moral virtues reinforce and complement each other; they are mutually interdependent. The natural virtues are *not* unified. An individual's charitable nature may override considerations of justice or desert an issue in an exaggerated willingness to excuse the wrongdoing of others. Or one may be naturally inclined to accept unreasonable risks, as a kind of meritorious recklessness. People's moderation in appetites may have little to do with an understanding of their needs and goods. They may just not have particularly strong desires of any kind, though this moderation may not extend across other dimensions of character.

In each case the person has a good quality and it may or may not be tarnished by the presence or absence of some other qualities. Someone could, I suppose, be a good person "all around" through natural virtue. But natural virtues are lesser than moral virtues in that they lack mutual reinforcement and orientation. Which one prevails will be a matter of the relative strength of factors not determined by right judgment and exertion. The moral virtues do complement, complete, and direct each other. They are not one but they are unified. The morally virtuous individual has attained a right conception of ends and the means to realize them. The naturally virtuous individual has not. Again, the contrast does not turn on inclinations being more labile or unreliable than moral virtues. The main point of contrast is that moral virtue reflects a level of agency that involves understanding and self-determination engaged to understanding that is absent from action grounded in natural inclination.

Perhaps it is because the moral virtues are unified that it is so *hard* to be good. They involve a complex repertoire of judgments, dispositions, and motives. No one of them can be complete on its own and we can't come to have them simply by decision. One can try to be more courageous but can't just bring it about by internal command. Self-imposition involves choice but is not simply choice. The point here is not just "what good is justice if you're too much of a coward to do the just thing?" That way of putting it confuses the issue a bit. If you *are* too much of a coward then whatever the quality of your judgment and understanding, you don't have the virtue of justice. Sometimes action may not involve strenuous or obvious demands upon more than one virtue. It may seem to be a straightforward matter of how courageous, temperate, honest, or just one is, for example, but a closer examination of cases indicates that several of these characteristics are involved. Consider the following. Suppose you are at a meeting, seminar, or presentation. The person speaking is well known, respected, and has a formidable presence. But it is clear to you that something important she or he claimed is quite wrong, and you know why. Others in the audience have either failed to notice the error or are too intimidated to point it out, though it is important. You sit there trying to decide whether to say something or not. You think of all sorts of reasons not to: it would be presumptuous or someone else will eventually make the point or you think "what's the big deal? It's not as if *I'm* being personally challenged," and so forth. Here it may look as if it were just a matter of courage. But I believe it is more complex than that. If it is not a context where *any* criticism is regarded as hostile and the objector's position or reputation is put at serious risk, there really is not a good reason to remain silent. It might take courage but it is also the fair and proper thing to do. The speaker and the audience would be served by having the error exposed and corrected, and so would you. After all, you are present at the gathering because the issues being discussed interest you and matter to you. It would be not only a bit cowardly, but also dishonest and unfair to hide behind rationalizations for keeping silent. Worries of this kind might well bother you (with reason) if you applaud and walk away without having spoken up. I don't mean to exaggerate the extent or degree of the failure here. This can be plausibly rendered as an episode of weakness or indecision rather than evidence of poor character. At the least it would be illustrative of the unity of weakness: that weakness, like virtue and vice, is multi-dimensional.

In fact, examination reveals that it would be very hard to diagnose any failure or lack of virtue as "simple" or one dimensional. These failures are easily and often *described* that way because one or another feature is outstanding or the focus of interest. But, in fact, a person is *not* just plain mean, selfish, or cowardly. Each of these vices is a multiple failure or lack. Their being identified as this or that specific vice is a matter of focus on the morally dominant features of the act or situation. It is instructive to consider the virtues as aspects of a unity rather than as independent, unrelated characteristics that may co-occur in some people. While some illustrations of the unity thesis may seem forced or implausible it seems to me much less plausible that each of the virtues could be present and effective on its own.

I think it is not very problematic to see how a particular vice can undermine or corrupt some other virtue. For example, the coward may not be able to get himself to perform what justice demands. Or, the individual lacking in knowledge of goods and needs may not have a sound grasp of what temperance would involve. Here it is (at least partly) because he doesn't know what's good for him that he acts badly, though not exclusively through incontinence or deliberate wrongful choice of the pleasurable over the good. But the claim I am arguing for is a bit different from this. It is not that the presence of a given vice is likely to lead to other modes of corruption. Rather, it is that *any* vice already involves manifold corruption. Here it might be objected that a moral vice does not extensively involve other moral defects but that it just makes the other virtues harder to attain and sustain.

I have a two-fold response to this suggestion. First, it seems clear that prudence is involved in all of the moral virtues since without the orientation it provides they cannot be effectively exercised. We need our action-guiding characteristics to be engaged to right ends. The claim that practical wisdom has a focal place among the virtues is found in many theories of them. Socrates, in the *Meno* says: "All spiritual qualities in and by themselves are neither advantageous nor harmful, but become advantageous or harmful by the presence with them of wisdom or folly."[8] And Epicurus writes: "For from prudence are sprung all the other virtues, and it teaches us that it is not possible to live pleasantly without living prudently and honorably and justly."[9] And Aristotle says: "It is not possible to be good in the strict sense without practical wisdom, nor practically wise without virtue,"[10] and "for with the presence of the one quality, practical wisdom, will be given all the virtues."[11] And Aquinas writes: "Prudence is absolutely the principal of all the virtues. The others are principal, each in its own genus."[12]

In each of these accounts of the virtues practical wisdom is the unifying and regulating virtue. It would not be effectively practical if not engaged to the other virtues, and they would not be proper moral virtues without being engaged to it. One might argue that whatever virtue a person has he or she must also have at least practical wisdom. This would not be the full strength unity thesis, but it would acknowledge that any virtue needs to be directed by prudence. More of an argument is needed to connect all of the virtues to each other.

The second part of my response is that the objection is correct that one sort of moral defect does make the other virtues harder, but one vice does not only make virtue harder, it really does include defects across the other moral dimensions. Cowardice is not just an impediment to being just. Injustice is ingredient in cowardice in that the latter prevents one from facing reasonable risks and the service of justice often requires that we do just that. To succumb to fear is to disengage oneself from doing what is owed to others and even oneself.

To illustrate these claims about unity, let us compare the moral virtues with physical virtues. An athlete may have the virtue of speed but may very well lack the virtues of strength, stamina, agility. But through effort he can develop his strength, agility, and stamina, which in the end will also reinforce and better enable him to use his speed. By vigorous conditioning and good habits, the athlete not only becomes stronger, but becomes faster, has more stamina, and is more agile. And if by lack of proper conditioning and bad habits the athlete's physical strength deteriorates significantly, so will his other physical virtues. The whole physical organism will deteriorate and the unity of the deterioration will be related to the severity of the deterioration of the one focal capacity. If the deterioration of strength is

---

[8]Plato *Meno*, 88D. translated by W.K.C. Guthrie, in *The Collected Dialogues of Plato* ed. by E. Hamilton and H. Cairns, Princeton Univ. Press, Princeton, NJ, 1963.

[9]From *The Stoic and Epicurean Philosophers*, ed. J. Oates, Random House, New York, NY, 1940, p. 32.

[10]1144b 30–31. Aristotle, *Nicomachean Ethics*.

[11]1145a 1–3. Aristotle, *Nicomachean Ethics*.

[12]*Summa Theologica*, Question 61, Article 2, Reply to Objection 1.

slight, the effects on speed, agility, and stamina may well be slight or even imperceptible. But a significant deterioration in any one cardinal capacity will inevitably result in an extensive failure of physical virtue.

Don't we find the same result with the moral virtues? Namely, defect in one respect extends throughout a repertoire of capacities and characteristics. Especially when a vice is present to a high degree the moral character as a complex whole is degraded. The effect of lesser degrees of vice may be small and even imperceptible. The general issue of specifying boundaries between vices and virtues is a difficult and imprecise one, and it can sometimes be difficult to judge the presence of a vice. But the larger danger is that one may recognize a vice, regard it (even if correctly) as slight, and accept it, be willing to "live with it." The problem is not that he is not fanatical enough in eradicating every trace of vice. I don't mean *that*. Rather, it is the idea that his character can be compartmentalized, and one or another feature of it can be safely confined and kept out of traffic with the others. Consider the individual who seems to exhibit justice, courage, and prudence but is intemperate. He regards his intemperance as tolerable in the respect that it does not undermine his good characteristics. But one cannot isolate intemperance in that way, or fix it to only certain objects, such as drugs, food, or what have you. I think there is a tendency to think of virtues and vices as correlated with certain typical objects or behaviors. To an extent this is correct, but it is a mistake if it is elevated to the status of a conceptual truth or completely reliable generalization. There is, upon examination, something odd about saying, for example, "he's just, courageous and prudent; he's just drunk too much of the time." If he drinks too much he allows his intemperance to degrade all of his capacities for right action. He is imprudent and also unfair to himself and others by being drunk when he should be sober, and so forth. His weakness for alcohol is not a tolerable cost in the context of the value of his virtues. It is in itself a drain on those assets. To tolerate it rather than employ his other resources to overcome it is to allow it to further undermine his virtues.

To say that any vice is extensive in the sense that it involves other vices is not to say that a person who is vicious at all is altogether vicious. A person can have one or another vice in the sense that his moral failings are typically of one or another kind. So, if someone is characteristically intemperate it does not follow that he or she is also characteristically unjust, imprudent, cowardly, and so on, any more than it follows that if someone is not quick they are a clumsy weakling. But their vice of intemperance involves failures of the other fundamental virtues.[13] Each characteristic may be present in varying degrees but a person's moral character is a complex unity. In this unity the condition of each virtue is interconnected with the others.

---

[13]This conception of the unity of virtues was developed with John Zeis. I owe the example comparing moral virtues to physical virtues to him.

If virtue and vice are unified and extensive in the respect that they involve complex, multiple exercises (or failures) of powers, then there is an important consequence for the relation of moral character to self-knowledge. The virtues just are certain orderings of the power of agency. Because virtue is unified and vice is unified, self-understanding cannot be compartmentalized. It too is extensive, or unified, because it is an appreciation of the mode of operation of one's agency. Here is a case where the character of understanding conforms in an important way to the character of its object. Unity in the exercise of one's power of self-determination facilitates unity in the understanding of one's motives, choices, and actions.

Self-knowledge follows self-mastery. The former is not merely a matter of knowing a good deal *about* oneself. That sort of knowledge is available in abundance to even the most morally depraved person. The speeches and writings of Hitler give ample evidence that he had a good, firm grip on what he was about. Self-knowledge, though, involves depth as well as quantity. A person can have much of the latter but be woefully lacking in the former. Sometimes what one knows about oneself can frighten the individual out of seeking self-knowledge. We may find ourselves repellent. Self-knowledge involves insight into the character and interrelations of the heterogeneous factors that together motivate and structure thought and action.

This type of knowledge is peculiarly accessible to the virtuous person. The operation of agency is self-disclosing in the respect that the explanation of action is present in it as the reasons that guide it. Even for the virtuous individual reflection and judgment about what to do are often needed. Other causal influences may be present but their efficacy is overridden. The agent can explain his action in terms of the reasons that determine it to be the right action. These reasons reflect components of a judgment that the individual makes and not causes that operate in or on him. To direct the exercise of one's capacities for thought and action in a virtuous manner is the most complete operation of constructive practical rationality. When actions are governed by *rational* causality there is no distance between their causality and their justification. What is moving the agent is a conception of what is required to act rightly. The power of rational conception through which the person perceives the situation may be employed practically as agency. This is the respect in which prudence is *practical* wisdom.

One final observation about the relation of virtue to self-knowledge. In matters of morality as in many other matters, people typically like what they are accustomed to. And what they are accustomed to is a result of circumstances, habituation, and example at least as much as deliberate choice. What is familiar supplies us with standards of interpretation, evaluation, and decision. So we can easily imagine people raised in moral beliefs and practices that do not conform well at all with even a very broad and flexible understanding of virtue, but to them they seem altogether fitting and correct. This issue raises concerns about relativism that I will have more to say about in the conclusion. The point here is that a set of beliefs and practices not subject to criticism and dispute (and perhaps even if they are) can become so firmly entrenched as a second nature that their nature doesn't seem to be secondary at all. To the individuals who have and engage in these beliefs and practices it may be evident and unproblematic that "this is what we do," or "this is what one does." Other views and activities may seem somehow less than fully genuine, as foreign currency doesn't seem like "real" money to many people. But familiarity and tenure of establishment are not reliable signs of the morality of beliefs and practices. They may not even be reliable signs of their intelligibility. I do not mean that we would find it difficult to identify or describe them. Rather, the reasons for them would be obscure and uncertain, in the sense that no adequate explanation in terms of constructive rationality is producible. Like certain matters of etiquette, they may come to have a place in our practical life that seems altogether natural. But even an illuminating causal explanation of their occurrence and persistence will not explicate them in moral terms. Indeed, it may turn out that the better we understand their genealogy the clearer it is that these beliefs and practices are immoral or morally inadequate. Cannibalism, sexual relations between adults and children, mutilation punishments for petty crimes, and slavery are fairly non-controversial examples of these points.

These observations indicate again that what takes the place of rational agency or constructive practical reasoning may easily be mistaken for them. People's beliefs, attitudes, and practices may be immoral, may conflict starkly with human goods and needs, but this does not imply that they will feel discomfort with them. They may be prized and tenaciously held. One may know in detail what "one does" and in what circumstances and with what sort of rationale. But even this knowledge may be superficial in the sense that it supplies a fragment of the anthropology of one's morality without indicating reasons that morally validate it.

Chapter 4

Critiques of Rational Self-Mastery

I have argued that virtue is an expression of one's nature as a self-determining being, and that it conduces to self-knowledge and self-enjoyment.
The ties to Aristotle and Kant bind this view of what it is to be moral and
what it is like to be moral to the special value of rational self-mastery. But
the view that a moral individual is a rationally well-ordered being who, as
such, realizes a genuine good for himself has been subject to sustained and
vigorous critique. I am not referring to Hume, the Utilitarians, or the
Emotivists. Rather, I have in mind those philosophers and literary figures
who have sought to convince us through argument and art that freedom
and self-knowledge are deeply problematic and ambiguous. Especially
from the mid nineteenth century to the present, there has been a growing
recognition or at least insistence that the view of rationally regulated self-
determination is overly optimistic. One primary reason for this is the view
that the conception of freedom as essentially rationally regulated is a fic-
tion. If we look, for example, at Kierkegaard, Nietzsche, Conrad, Gide, and
Camus among others we find that there is still a deep tie between freedom,
morality, and self-knowledge. But it is not the one we have described. It is
still the core issue, but it is so because it is so fully problematic, not because
it is unequivocal. If human nature has no intrinsic end, which is formally
similar and objectively identifiable across persons, then our self-determina-

tion is not oriented to a fixed, knowable target. It is more like a power which must seek direction and an end than a potentiality which realizes an end which is intrinsic to it. Indeed, this raises the question whether self-determination is even rationally regulated. Why is reason to be prized when we are called by and must answer to so much else in ourselves? One way to formulate this altered problematic is, "why is rational self-determination the prior need and goal, when there is so much else that is needed in discovering and constructing our individuality?" Could not valuing this lead more to repression, inhibition, and self-deception than to expression or well-ordering of our nature? Isn't rational self-mastery just one choice, one option as a mode of freedom? While we may *prefer* it, are there really decisive grounds to think it *best*?

The point here is not that there is some specific alternative candidate that we have ignored or discounted. The point is that there is no privileged end for freedom at all. To be free or to accept one's freedom is to acknowledge possibility: the possibility of a variety of acknowledgements of one's needs, drives, abilities, commitments, and projects. And it is *always* this way. It is not as if the mature, reflective individual achieves a stable state of practical wisdom that with a calm but powerful inertia guides him to self-enjoyment through virtue. We have no right to be so optimistic.

The authors I have mentioned are but a few of a large number of influential thinkers who investigated and articulated these concerns. The main theme of the grouping is the ambiguity of freedom, moral identity, and moral value, once the regulative authority of reason is questioned or denied. It is not enough for the denial to be simply cranky or motivated by an unwillingness to accept the discipline of responsibility for oneself. And the most important denials were not simply cranky. They were a challenge to the notion that responsibility for oneself led *one* way, as it were. The critics accepted the responsibility but were less confident that it was a means to a conception of self-realization for persons that applied generally and cut across individual variability by being grounded in our nature. The two main charges of these "rival" views as I shall discuss them here are (i) that self-determination and integrity of personality are perhaps considerably more complex and equivocal than the portrayal of them in some versions of the rational self-mastery view; and (ii) that, additionally, it is unclear that self-determination has an end specific to it, well-fitted to it, the realization of which is constitutive of something like self-enjoyment. Even if we maintain that rational self-mastery is an intrinsic and valuable end for persons, given their nature, much of the content of the first charge must be accommodated. There is no clean break between the rational and irrational, no hard and fast compartmentalization of the character of motivations. Moreover, people's needs, drives, and deepest impulses are different. Thus, on the rival views what counts as genuine self-determination will differ according to what it is that really expresses the individual. There is no guarantee that it is virtue in the sense of rational self-determination that unifies and informs expression of one's agency. It is helpful to observe how this shift away from rationally regulated self-determination alters the interpretation of weakness of will and vice.

In some strands of the critical alternative views weakness is reinterpreted as a refusal to acknowledge and accept one's impulses and needs, whether or not they conform to some alleged standards of virtue. In others, it is weakness and self-deception to even think there are any objectively justified or grounded virtues. Perhaps we all need courage just to carry on and live worthwhile lives in a precarious world. But it may be a kind of courage of authenticity that allows free play to passions, and impulses, and their interpretation unguided by principle. Creativity, or at least expression and assertion, replace control and mastery. To choose the latter is to indulge a deception that disguises what it fears. It is not necessarily a self-imposed process of successfully realizing one's nature. Rather, it is a choice of self-interpretation, but one without any credentials of privilege. The truest acknowledgement is that criteria of self-interpretation are subjective. This is not to say that they are arbitrary or capricious, but that they are not grounded in some shared nature. The account of rational self-determination and its relation to self-enjoyment did allow for individual variability. But it required that the former be attached to the latter through virtue, and it identified virtue with a certain sort of employment of agency, that is, agency guided by considerations of objective goods. So, it is really the character of agency, the manner in which it truly indicates the self which is at issue. In the next few pages I will discuss the critique of the rational self-mastery view by using illustrations from works by some of the authors I've mentioned. Kant, for example, would evaluate Michel in Gide's *Immoralist* as indeed being immoral. Aristotle would at least find him weak. And both would probably find the protagonist of Conrad's *Lord Jim* a self-absorbed egoist, not selfish in any crass way, but overly indulgent with an ideal he cannot distinguish from fantasy. But both Gide and Conrad do succeed in portraying the ambiguity and anxiety that attends self-determination. Their leading characters are not straightforward examples of people who fall short of practical wisdom and thus make mistakes that undo them. They are examples of the opacity and obstacles inherent in the struggle to interpret and orient oneself.

It would be a crude mistake to see Gide's Michel as an example of what can "go wrong" when one struggles to free oneself from the restraints and guidance of moral principles and habits. (Not that he was a good example of virtue in the first place.) Anyway, he is not someone gleefully casting off the discipline of morality and indulging in vice. He is someone who is slowly, uncertainly beginning to acknowledge impulses, desires, and sensibilities that had been latent or repressed. Through the course of his illness and his awakening sensibility, he comes to regard his past as repressed, philistine, and life-denying. The changes he undergoes in his own self-conceptions and in the ways he sees his wife and others "grow" on and in him more than they are the result of reflection. It is quite a while before he has anything like an appreciation of the changes he is undergoing. He does not have a plan for rebellion and a conception of a new order for his life. He exhibits nothing like that much deliberateness and intentionality. That, I think, is part of what is more important in trying to understand him.

The difficulty of freedom is these alternative views is not in freeing oneself *from* passions, selfish interests, and impulses, as in the mastery view. This is how Kant, for example, sees the issue. But this rationality-versus-pathology conception of the problem is too narrow: narrow to the point of deception. The deception is that there is a normatively privileged manner of organizing one's thought and action, and that the means to it is to fashion a character as free as possible from the interference of non-agent causes. But this rival view challenges the notion that this should be the focus of moral and practical attention. There is much else to attend to with at least as strong claims on us.

The self-mastery model involves something like an ideal of orderliness: the elimination of various types of motives, or at least the minimization of their efficacy. Mastery is control authorized and enforced by agency.[1] But from the perspective of many of the critical views the authority of rational agency disfigures and represses the self. It legislates confines for self-determination. If we look at the writings of the critics of the rational self-mastery view we do not find a well-defined rival conception of the result of self-determination when it is exercised to the full. But this is not a defect of their views, it is its point. Freedom is essentially ambiguous and therefore so is morality and the self. The ambiguity can be resolved by choice and orientation, but never with definite correctness. And so freedom is a tangled web of rebellion, discovery, commitment, revision, and experimentation. The character of the self cannot be discerned by inspection and observation or a sorting of motives into preclassified types. It is good to find one's way, to come to terms with one's nature, but we may find that kind of stability to be elusive, or might even find our way but without the security of thinking it good. The critiques did not turn primarily on disputes about the right construal of rationality. Their approach was different. They raised the concern of whether rationality, in whatever preferred version, had or should have regulative authority.

The optimism of the self-mastery view consists in its theses that there

---

[1] As Kant puts it in the *Foundations of the Metaphysics of Morals*:

> The inclinations themselves as the sources of needs, however, are so lacking in absolute worth that the universal wish of every rational being must be indeed to free himself completely from them.

Trans. L. W. Beck, Bobbs-Merrill Company, Inc., Indianapolis, IN, 1959, p. 46.

is an end for persons given their nature, and that to realize this end maximally *is* good. But like most philosophical theories it oversimplifies, is reductionist in a sense, and to that extent it falsifies. Its Aristotelian dimension is too sure that self-mastery is essentially a rationally regulated activity that is constitutive of happiness. The Kantian dimension of it is too sure that non-rational sources of motivation are both inferior and (to a sufficient extent, anyway) manageable. The rival views, lacking both of these grounds of confidence, reject the guiding image. The rival views refuse to appeal to that guiding image in order to validate self-interpretations. They are not satisfied that self-determination conduces to an end, self-enjoyment, that is intrinsic to our nature.

On the self-mastery view maximization of rationality is a success notion tied to an ideal. If authenticity or some cognate notion replaces or displaces agency then it is uncertain whether even being rationally well-ordered is an appropriate and desirable end. Michel in the *Immoralist* is quite un-well-ordered at the end of the story. But the point is not that he has gone wrong or become undone. It is that he has had to face up to unstable and conflicting acknowledgments. He has enriched and improved his self-interpretation. But the enrichment has not resulted in unimpeded virtuous activity that is naturally pleasing and transparent in its motivational character. He has shed roles, habits, and illusions inculcated by upbringing, experience, and unreflective commitments. But the loss, which is welcome, is not automatically compensated for by a gain which is equally or more welcome. Part of the explanation for this is that even habits, roles, and commitments that have been shed cast a lingering shadow, and one's identification with them is not totally undone. Their inertia continues to have an influence. But the other part of the explanation is that it is never obvious what should replace them. The very realization of freedom is anxiety producing and painful. Michel remains a stranger to himself to the extent that he is aware of the possibilities of his freedom. He is aware of and responsive to the powers of both conscience and passion, his vocation and his sensuality, his responsibilities to his wife and his desire to focus his energies on the transformation of his own personality. The categories and vocabulary of self-interpretation have changed. He doesn't see the issue as a battle between virtue and responsibility on the one hand and selfish indulgence and spontaneity of instinct on the other. He has *already* extricated himself from this view of his situation and he regards having done so as an affirmation of his self. But because the dilemma has dissolved, his choices and manner of carrying on are not automatically determined by rejection of one or the other side of it. And so, as he says toward the very end of the book, "This useless freedom tortures me."[2]

The idea that freedom is tormenting is completely alien to the

---

[2]A. Gide, *The Immoralist*, tr. R. Howard, Vintage Books, New York, NY, 1970, p. 169.

rational self-mastery view. There, it is unfreedom that is painful, threatening, and corrosive of self-respect. To be unfree is a kind of mismanagement with deleterious effects. It is not part of that view that freedom could itself be disorderly. But one's most honest self-interpretation may show that it is necessary to hold onto extremes for which there is no satisfactory mean. To seek a mean or mastery over one or another extreme would itself be a defect in self-understanding. It is a denial that can take the form of repression without dissolving and vitiating what is repressed.[3] The transparency of what is repressed is clouded, but its causality is not diminished. But what is repressed is not just an impulse or urge that offends the conscience or is incongruous with a self-conception, it may be a conception of the self, a dimension of purposiveness and fulfillment that is no less *really* part of the self and essential to its interpretation.

What must I include, express, and give affective and motivational play to in order to realize and sustain my integrity? In a sense, integrity may seem to be a conservative notion. That is, it involves stability, equilibrium, and adaptation, as it were, without trauma or radical change. At least in its moral exemplification it has been widely thought to involve *fixity* of character. But is integrity of personality something one can attain without equilibrium or stability? Are honesty about and honest expression of the self something that may conflict with stability or regularity of pattern of thought and action? In the *Immoralist*, for example, Michel holds on to extremes he finds in himself, and the result is an amalgam of creative discovery and self-destruction. His self-realization consists in large part of acceptance of incongruous drives and needs and confusion about how to proceed.[4] His "old" integrity is shattered; his "new" integrity is not fully formed, and the book ends with indications that it is not likely to be. But what has been repressed has surfaced, what had formerly been in control has had its authority challenged. There is a sense in which Michel's integrity has come apart. But there is also a sense in which his very vulnerability marks an increase in integrity. He is at least willing to give attention to things in himself that he would formerly have denied or repressed as scandalous and improper. Each different side is dominant in turn and is then restrained by the other, leaving him in an unrelieved tension of opposites. A new consolidation of personality does not take place and is not promised. There is no assurance of a stable state of self-interpretation, because there is no assurance of a stable vocabulary and ensemble of concepts that determine normative judgments of the self. This is a painful and perplexing condition to be in. People have different sorts of energy. They

[3]As Michel says near the end of the book:
> Sometimes I'm afraid that what I have suppressed will take its revenge. I want to make a fresh start.

A. Gide, *The Immoralist*, tr. R. Howard, Vintage Books, New York, 1970, p. 171.
[4]Ibid, especially pp. 169–170.

have intellectual, emotional, and creative energies that all demand attention and engagement and may not interact or reinforce each other harmoniously. A person has to acknowledge the force and direction of these types of energy and also make choices about channeling, committing, and restraining them.

On these rival views, elements of personality that the self-mastery view interprets as problematic and threatening to self-determination and integrity of personality are incorporated into the latter as no less legitimate than rational regulation. It is not what threatens freedom that is problematic; freedom itself is. If a person examines her ends, interests, and values, she will see that many of them are shaped by roles, habituation, and a rich and varied context of conventions. These may be sincerely or insincerely, willingly or unwillingly, deeply or superficially, inculcated and internalized. Some are internalized by choice; many are not. A critical examination of them, one that penetrates them, will "see through" many of them as persisting simply through familiarity or security with an established pattern of dispositions and motives. To raise questions about them, about the extent to which they are genuine expressions of self-interpretation can undermine them. This is not inevitable, but it is surely possible. One can then begin to make those fine but significant distinctions between ends, ideals, deceptions, and fantasies. It may be that the latter two are overrepresented in oneself. One can then choose to live with an excess of deception and fantasy or try to alter the situation. But in any case it is possible not only to apply an apparatus of evaluative concepts to oneself but also to assess the apparatus. And this is where freedom is problematic not just with respect to how well the individual "lives up to" her standards and ideals, but with respect to what those standards and their ground should be.

This is an issue on which the critical views are willing to accommodate two different outcomes that the rational self-mastery view rejects. The first is that the exercise of one's freedom may not have much or at least anything essential to do with moral virtue as I have explicated it, borrowing from Aristotle and Kant. One's freedom may involve liberation from the authority of rational standards of self-determination. One's agency is found in other sources of motivation. The second is that one's freedom may remain problematic, equivocal, and conflicted if opposing needs and potentials are found in one's deepest self-appreciation. In either case the optimism grounded in the agency-unity-virtue relation is overthrown. We do not know ourselves as transparently as that view would have us believe. We do not so much fashion our self-determination along certain lines intrinsic to our nature, but instead we develop it originally through experience, interpretation, and opportunity.

Perhaps the focal issue in this clash of views is the question of what one's agency consists in. Is it realizing one's nature as a member of an objectively characterizable kind, as a rational agent approximating to an ideal defined by the perfection of certain capacities? Or, is it realizing one's nature as an individual without any sort of end or good fixed by a nature common with other members of the kind? Indeed, it may seem that the answer to *this* dilemma is a matter of self-interpretation, not metaphysics or a general philosophical psychology. It is easy to multiply examples in support of either case: examples of how supposed virtue is repressive and leads to inner divisions and conflicts, and examples of how rationally unregulated freedom culminates in despair and self-destruction. Freedom without direction is not freedom, but rather a kind of indulgent self-assertion.

Both sides in this dispute tend to caricature the other. As I have argued, virtue is not a matter of being confined by self-restraint and self-denial. It does involve denying efficacy to certain kinds of motives, but its aim is not that the individual constrict and inhibit himself. If this were the case, then the relation to self-enjoyment would be completely implausible. The notion of self-enjoyment is certainly not just a negative notion of freedom *from* motives and impulses that interfere with moral virtue. It needn't be construed as austere, or requiring the sorts of deliberateness and self-scrutiny in action that wreck spontaneity and naturalness. On the other side, neither should dropping the requirement of rational regulation in self-determination be regarded as tantamount to an anarchy issuing in despair and degradation. The alternative is not just being "carried away" or yielding to every impulse and opportunity for pleasure, but as the critiques indicate, a plasticity and openness in agency that are foreign to the rational self-mastery view are available to us.

According to many of these critical views freedom has no intrinsic, "natural" direction. Because of this it is not crucial to develop dispositions that tend toward the maximization of rational agency. Nor is assimilation and appreciation of the past quite as important. One's past, whether well understood or not, will still have important influences on abilities, attitudes, and the various dimensions of character. But there is less of a concern with the cultivation of self-understanding with a view to a specific end. It is plain that in *Lord Jim*, Jim's past is extremely important to him. But in *The Immoralist* and *The Stranger*, disengagement from the burden of the past is advocated. Menalque in *The Immoralist* explains that he has no interest in writing his memoirs because:

> If I did, I might keep the future from happening by letting the past encroach upon it. I create each hour's newness by forgetting yesterday completely. *Having been* happy is never enough for me. I don't believe in dead things.[5]

And in *The Stranger*, Meursault while listening to the prosecutor finish the

---

[5]Ibid, p. 111.

details of imposing upon him a character he did not recognize as his own at all, says to himself:

> Still, to my mind he overdid it, and I'd have liked to have a chance of explaining to him, in a quite friendly, almost affectionate way, that I have never been able really to regret anything in all my life. I've always been far too much absorbed in the present moment or the immediate future, to think back.[6]

To someone who does not regard freedom as a power of regulatively directing one's life according to objective considerations, unity will be relatively less important because its significance is in how it helps to clarify and delineate the scope and power of one's rational agency. The ideals of unity and self-knowledge are stripped of their attractions if rational self-mastery is denied to be the end. To the critic of rational self-mastery it need not follow that the rejection of rationally regulating one's life involves forfeiting self-mastery. One could regard freedom from reason as a kind of mastery. But I will try to explain below why rationality and unity are crucial to self-mastery.

The critical views take moral virtue, in that it is rationally regulated, as an artificial, constraining construct. The cultivation of a moral character guided by rational considerations, therefore, seems forced and partial, leaving out or suppressing other drives and sensibilities. It is an imposition of limits determined by artificial standards. The removal of these limits, pulling down barriers to individual self-expression and assertion, is no guarantee that one's life will be transformed into a harmony of satisfactions and gratifying self-realizations. But self-expression or self-expansion is at least a more natural and authentic manner of self-determination than the appropriation of standards and limits not themselves determined by felt need or instinct. This is not natural virtue if we mean by that unreflective, untrained activity that happens to conform to rationally governed moral virtue. It is not, or need not be, part of this view that unfettered self-expression and disclosure are the most effective means to the realization of some true human good. That idea is perhaps more like views sometimes expressed by some of the Lake Poets and their faith in the intrinsic goodness of human desires. Wordsworth, for example, writes:

> his noble nature, as it is
> The gift which God has placed
> within his power,
> His blind desires and steady faculties
> capable of clear truth, the one to break
> Bondage, the other to build liberty
> On firm foundations.[7]

[6]A. Camus, *The Stranger*, tr. S. Gilbert, Vintage Books, New York, NY, 1946, pp. 126–127.

[7]*Poems of William Wordsworth*, ed. N. C. Smith, 1908, Prelude, Bk. IX, 355–60.

And Thelwall, echoing the theme of the natural ability of man writes:

That thus, as with all I alternately blend,
The *mind* may expand and the *heart* may amend;
Till, embracing Mankind in one girdle of Love,
In Nature's kind lesson I daily improve,
And (no haughty distinctions to fetter my soul)
As the brother of all, learn to feel for the whole.[8]

These and other Romantics thus promulgated something like a doctrine of *natural* virtue, putting their faith in nature not corrupted and disfigured by reason and political and social convention and contrivance. In their view self-expression revealed a real underlying goodness. But it seems to be part of many of the later views that self-expression and disclosure are the primary values *because* there is no specific true human good. Our freedom *is* our end. The point of liberating oneself is to escape unfreedom. It is not that freedom makes accessible some further prize, such as self-enjoyment or self-respect, social harmony, and welfare. It *may*, and if there is happiness in life it is happiness attained through an unconstrained disclosure of one's individuality. Freedom is not without value. Indeed it just is the possibility of self-cultivation and creation of value.

There have been many different resolutions to the problem of freedom as thus characterized. They hardly need labels, since the famous names attached to them are so rich in associations and implications. I have in mind Nietzsche, Kierkegaard, Dostoevsky, Gide, Camus, and Sartre among others. The names I have listed surely do not constitute a school. But they indicate approaches to or out of the problem of individuality and freedom that the critique of rational self-mastery made inevitable. All of them wrestled with the issue of integrity of the self and its relation to morality, though there was nothing like the formulation of a new consensus.

One of the merits of the critiques of rational self-mastery was that they brought into bold relief a number of psychological and motivational issues that clearly had not received adequate recognition and attention. The various critiques and rejections of rational self-mastery broadened and deepened the notion of the self. They gathered into the central arena of selfhood elements of what to Kant, at least, were heteronomy and pathology. This is reflected in the use of metaphors of health or flourishing and sickness. The flourishing involved giving free play to the needs, drives, and impulses that are the sources of motivation that rational self-mastery sought to dominate. It is unhealthy to suppress what energizes and satisfies.

[8]J. Thelwall, *The Peripatetic* (1973) Vol ii, p 228. John Thelwall was a revolutionary enthusiast tried (and acquitted) in the State Trials of 1794.

This is not a matter of simply unleashing forces hitherto checked by conscience, but of actualizing the variety of motives that we are susceptible to. It would be inaccurate to portray this as a license for flaunting depravity. The point is that this is how a person honestly and sincerely presents his individuality. Rational self-mastery may be at odds with integrity and authenticity.

We can no longer see the problem of freedom and the dynamics of moral motivation as a conflict between two distinct, sharply contrasted sources of motivation such as reason and appetite. The nineteenth and twentieth century authors mentioned looked deeply into *levels* of motivation and metaphors of surface and depth took on increasing significance. Our motivational situation is not like a plain on which are arrayed two opposing armies that can see each other clearly and watch each other's movements. And so the strategy of freedom is found to be considerably more complicated than it seemed before. Notions such as repression, self-deception, sublimation, and others that are, so to speak, "vertical" in application add a new dimension. We often don't see our motives and needs clearly, and they can be hidden under layers of defenses, denial, and concealment that while self-imposed, have a logic that operates without conscious control, but is still reflected in personality, character, thought, and action.

The difficulty of self-determination is not just that we might be weak against what opposes reason but also that influential factors are often hidden and we are partly responsible for concealing them. We make many of the enemies of our own freedom though we are not always aware of doing so. From Kant and Aristotle we get little indication of the dimensions of difficulty and types of obscurity in self-understanding. Kant allows that we can never be sure of the purity of our motives, but this is because of the location of pure practical reason in the noumenal realm, not because sources of irrational causality are hidden. They are *always* present, since the "dear self" is always present. But this is a somewhat different and less complex (if no less severe) worry than the other theorists were exercised by. They indicated the various ways in which the consolidation of personality along lines of rational self-mastery could always be vulnerable to being undone. So, even if this is the model of self-determination one strives to realize, it may never become so secure that it is not questioned and successfully challenged by events and experiences. Lord Jim for example, is a fellow who is undone by an event, his leaving the Patna. And while he spends the rest of his life (*and* his death) dedicated to reconstituting his integrity along the favored lines of his youth, it is not at all clear whether he succeeds. We can alternately interpret him as self-indulgent and self-deluded or as showing admirable and courageous resolve in committing himself and sacrificing himself to an ideal. But the ambiguity is not just in interpreting the results. It is also in understanding what it is in himself that this dedication and commitment answer to.[9] He certainly has deliberateness and determination, and it is plain that what moves him exerts a great deal of pressure on him. But we are never quite sure in Jim's case just what the task is and whether it is one he has undertaken or one that drags or pushes him along.

Our motives and goals do not come to us labelled as rational or not. The classification and judgement are a result of self-scrutiny, and how they square with our plans, interests, and self-conceptions. Of course, not even Kant thought it was easy to consolidate one's personality along lines of rational self-mastery. It is very difficult and requires a great deal of exertion and conscientious attention. But this is more a difficulty of effort than of interpretation and understanding. At least his statement of what self-determination requires suggests simplicity of a sort, if not ease of execution. Aristotle's psychology, as indicated by the ethical treatises and the *Rhetoric* was a good deal more empirically and phenomenologically plausible, but still lacked in certain respects compensated for in the nineteenth and twentieth century critiques. But those critiques also overcompensated. In part, they were motivated by historical and contextual factors that we can hardly blame earlier theorists for not addressing. Kant, I believe, did anticipate some of them. He like many of his critics, was acutely concerned that persons should not be assimilated by causal-mechanical science into just another kind of natural object. He sought to preserve the intrinsic worth of persons through his metaphysic of rational nature wherein the causality of agency was not dissolved. But, as we remarked earlier, this involved a fatal detachment of moral personality from the world persons live and act in. The overcompensation of the rival critiques lay in exaggerating the ambiguity and formlessness of self-determination.

Part of this excess was the result of overextending self-determination through emphasis on self-interpretation. The range of things that might figure in self-interpretation was extended, partly through a critique of culture, partly through a heightened subjectivity. Philosophical interpretation of society and culture took on a character and vigor that are not found in either Aristotle or Kant. I imagine much of the impetus for this is owed to Nietzsche whose reevaluation of values involved an emphasis on revealing the historical psychology of moral theorizing. He altered the terms of evaluation and brought a powerful new perspective to thinking about both moral phenomena and moral theory. He was widely regarded as showing not only what the history of moral theory had made of itself but of men,

[9]The narrator, Marlow, seems not to settle on any definitive assessment of Jim's personality, and while there are at least half a dozen instances where he describes Jim as "one of us," there are several where he also describes him as "not clear to me," or an enigma, etc. For the former, see pages 38, 64, 75, 85, 244, 249. For the latter pages 136, 169, 253, in Penguin Modern Classic, New York, 1985.

and he was furious with the results. How the prevailing culture shaped and reflected the subject was important to many of the critics. The culture was roundly condemned for its shallow materialism, weakness of spirit, and tiresome, conventional, conformist values. Nietzsche condemned the herd instinct appropriate to the weak of spirit. Kierkegaard decried what he saw as a kind of bloodless objectivity. Others, both philosophical and literary saw it as a culture that repressed, corrupted, and enervated the will of the individual, to the point where acceptance of its lifeless, clumsy values threatened to extinguish the potential for human individuality and flourishing. Worst of all, most people, through a kind of conspiracy of weakness and false consciousness, accepted its terms of evaluation. These authors saw as one of their tasks and one of the tasks of morality the restoration of the individual, the rebirth of subjectivity, character, and commitment from the personal, internal point of view. This could not be facilitated by a reliance on or reformulation of rationality. That was the core of the "official doctrine" that oppressed them. The conception of self-determination had to be revised, the authority that justified its mode of operation relocated. Morality was an institutionalization of a kind of rationality that had lost its legitimacy.

Like most revolutions, this one went too far. The excess was not in overstating the responsibility of the self. The present account of rational self-mastery seeks to preserve that to a very high degree. The error was in rejecting the idea of a telos for self-determination, in rendering it aimless, by denying the presence of any authoritative criteria for its exercise. In a sense, some of the critics reversed the Aristotelian logic in which actuality is prior to potentiality and they made possibility prior to actuality. But it is possibility without any criteria of closure. And so it remains possibility and is disengaged from a conception of fulfillment or effective realization. The problem of self-determination was reformulated in a manner that did not admit of a solution. Nietzsche claimed to find a basis in the will to power for values that could not be rationally supported and happily went in for moral inequality and self-assertion by the members of a priesthood of bullies. Kierkegaard took a leap of faith that others hesitated to follow, and Sartre got nauseous. An account of rationally guided freedom could not get a foothold since it required some sort of conception of the nature of persons that was common, and not infinitely plastic and constantly altering. The critique made the problem of reconstituting the self nearly insoluble by rejecting criteria for how it ought to be. There is no compass to guide us in gaining perspective on what our integrity of personality or moral integrity consists in. And thus the absurd gains entry. There is no best way to see ourselves and questions of value.

This need not result in nihilism. One can make an affirmation, create a value or a perspective to unify, structure, and give point to one's freedom. But the affirmation, though internally motivated, is precarious. It is not a matter of seeing or finding that something is so and acknowledging it. It is an assertion shadowed by the awareness that merely asserting something does not make it so. But it indicates the truth that lest freedom dissolve into a pointless play of unregulated motivations, the agent must determine himself through articulating commitments. The main thrust of the rival theories as characterized here is that there is no particular commitment which is binding, demands attention, or counts as a right determination.

Sartre, for one, is sensitive to the charge that his existentialism is pessimistic in contrast to the optimism of the objectivist (or theist). He tries to show that optimism is with *his* philosophy, that "it is a doctrine of action, and it is only by self-deception, by confusing their own despair with ours that Christians can describe us as without hope."[10] He says this, in spite of the fact that his existentialism essentially involves anguish, abandonment, and despair. Respectively these are that "a man cannot escape from the sense of complete and profound responsibility";[11] that God does not exist and man "cannot find anything to depend upon whether within or outside himself";[12] and that "we limit ourselves to a reliance upon that which is within our wills, or within the sum of the probabilities which render our action feasible."[13] By this he seems to mean that there is no providential order or promised end, natural or divine, to guide choices and safeguard values.

Sartre wants to make clear that our having to "act without hope" is not a way of breaking us, dissolving commitment, vitiating action. It is to see the true, historical, lived human situation for what it is, that is, something we are radically responsible for. Thus he recasts the gloom into opportunity, the opportunity of thorough self-making and self-surpassing, the opportunity of making man and man's freedom the end that is still to be determined.

As should be clear, I think such a view is mistaken. I have discussed it because it does raise serious objections and because its variants have a good deal of currency. The main defect of the view is that in detaching self-

---

[10]"Existentialism is a Humanism," p. 369, reprinted in *Existentialism From Dostoevsky to Sartre*, ed. W. Kaufmann, New American Library, New York, 1975. And Nietzsche, in the early aftermath of the death of God, writes

It is perhaps that we are still too deeply impressed by the first consequences of this event—and these first consequences, the consequences for us, are perhaps the reverse of what one might expect: not at all sad and dark, but rather like a new, scarcely describable kind of light, happiness, relief, exhilaration, encouragement, dawn?

From "Fearlessness," in *The Gay Science, The Portable Nietzsche*, ed. and tr. W. Kaufmann, Viking Press, New York, NY, 1954, pp. 447–448.

[11]Sartre, "Existentialism is a Humanism," in *Existentialism from Dostoevsky to Sartre*, ed. W. Kaufmann, New American Library, New York, 1975. p. 351.

[12]Sartre, p. 353.

[13]Sartre, p. 357.

determination from an end, it dissolves self-determination and renders almost hopeless the task of self-interpretation. The view was not an *attack* on freedom or self-understanding, but a critique of a certain family of theories about them. But the critique devoured what it intended to save.

According to this view we no longer have a guiding conception, even in general terms, of what powers of self-determination are and what they ought to be aimed at. We still have a thorough-going responsibility for ourselves and an acknowledgement of the centrality of honestly facing up to the task of self-interpretation. But without a principle of unity and direction, our self-determination is rendered pointless. For those who stopped short of nihilism or despair it was better, and more humane, to regard our situation as an opportunity for reconstituting values in the clear knowledge that they are our own creations and do not reflect or attach to any transcendent or fixed grounding. This is to fully realize one's freedom as a potential for self-making, to translate the despair of seeming point-lessness into a prospect and an affirmation.

If we consider Conrad, Gide, and Camus we get a good, synoptic impression of the literary history of the breakdown of the teleological, rational self-mastery view. Through them we can also trace this critique through stages of ambiguity, anxiety, and absurdity and, finally, with Camus, a sort of affirmation, or at least the possibility of it. Camus, for example, regards suicide, nihilism, and the leap of faith as evasions or false solutions to the problem of freedom. The evacuation of metaphysical meaning from the world will not accommodate just any replacement. But perhaps by the time Camus was writing there was an awakening under-standing of how serious and threatening the ethical situation had become upon the dissolution of the older doctrines. Camus sought to reformulate a conception of human nature to help reorient moral thinking that had become badly disoriented. Camus' work is not a systematic elaboration of a theory. It is almost more of a plea put forward in the rich language of literary imagery and historical illustration. If there is no object for free-dom, no objective, fixed grounding for moral value at least there is a community of shared predicament. It is not so much the characteristics of our nature as persons that morally engage us to each other, it is our situa-tion.

I will not comment further on Camus except to observe that he is indicating how to be free without offering an intrinsic end for freedom. He rejects self-destructive despair, aestheticism, suicide, the leap of faith, and the will to power. He opts for solidarity based on human dignity. But whatever option one commits to, if freedom has no intrinsic end, an end must be supplied to it: an end that will lend unity and direction to self-determination and self-interpretation. Even if human nature has no intrin-sic teleology, man seeks and constructs a telos. Perhaps as Camus, Sartre, and others have urged, the world does not answer to the natural human tendency to seek unity and significance. Surely what we desire and what the world offers do not coincide. There isn't, according to them in addition to how things are, a way they ought to be that is discoverable or indicated by the facts of the world and our constitution. Nothing we could find out about the nature of the world could solve the problem of freedom. This is the lesson of the passage from ambiguity to anxiety to absurdity. But we must still make our freedom bearable, put it to work somehow, engage it to ends. This is exactly the issue people such as Camus and deBeauvoir present and address. The difficulty is not just how to cope, but how to put our individual freedom to work without illusion or evasion; how to be honest when the truth is something we can acknowledge only insofar as we also make it.

The idea of rational self-mastery as a constitutive means to virtue-generated self-enjoyment would seem to be a constriction of freedom. It puts a kind of limit or closure on self-determination and it is one possibility among others. This, at least, is a theme of many of its critics. Camus and de Beauvoir are two examples of those who, in coming to terms with the problematic nature of freedom, sought to reconnect it to morality. Freedom is not simply a power for originality, guiltless dissipation, and egoistic self-assertion. The freedom of others must be acknowledged, respected, and promoted.[14] So, unlike the Decadents, Nietzscheans, and some others, they affirmed a solution to the problem that tended in the direction of shared acknowledgments and community of moral concern. But this is not evidence that they simply reinstated a teleological theory of human nature.

Given the vigor and diversity of the critique of the teleological theory of human nature, it might seem that to advocate that theory is to repeat mistakes already well-documented. The issue here is to be able to distinguish how best to account for moral phenomena from how we prefer to account for them. A theory that involves a kind of rational essentialism that accounts for moral psychology and the unity of a personal history faces an uncongenial intellectual environment. Central to it is the idea that what persons are reveals how they ought to be, that accurate description and explanation have normative significance. Critics as unsympathetic to each other as Hume and Ayer on the one hand and Nietzsche and the Existentialists on the other reject this. If there is moral value it is not to be found by reason. If there is a way persons ought to be, they make it so and do not discover it. In one respect, I concur with this. The transition from what we are to what we should be is not automatic or inevitable. It essentially involves striving, resolve, and exertion guided by reflection and deliberation. But I do think that there is such a thing as personal nature and that it

---

[14]de Beauvoir writes, "In the first place, it seems to us that the individual as such is one of the ends at which our action must aim. Here we are at one with the point of view of Christian charity, the Epicurean cult of friendship, and Kantian moralism which treats each man as an end." *The Ethic of Ambiguity*, Citadel Press, New York, NY, 1964, p. 135.

is best accounted for in terms of a network of interrelated capacities. While there may be difficulties in drawing a sharp line between persons and non-persons, I would argue that the distinction is real. It is something one can be correct or mistaken about. Moreover, I believe that what-it-is-to-be a person involves certain normative considerations. Bernard Williams in *Morality* discusses Aristotle's moral theory and criticizes it for taking rational capacities as somehow privileged and dominant. After all, he remarks, there are many regards in which humans are distinctive, in their ability to make fire, make love without regard to season, and to kill other creatures for fun.[15] He is right to reject the simple assertion that rationality, whether theoretical or practical, is obviously the locus of value or preeminent value. Since we are not fully governed by instinct, we *need* rationality. But we need many things and it is not obvious or irresistible that *rationality* embodies some sort of qualitative superiority. In any case, the very nature of rationality is much disputed.

Michel remarks at the end of the *Immoralist*, that useless freedom is torture. Self-determination needs a target, a direction, an orientation or it dissipates in ennui or worse. But how can one make out a case for *the* target for it? What would *show* that it is self-enjoyment, virtue, maximization of satisfactions, creativity, power, or any of the other candidates? Why should we think that there is any specific tendency which is especially appropriate, "natural," or normatively privileged?

The core of my answer to this question is that the need for unity imposes a requirement for self-determination to have an end. Unity is neither monotony, nor is it necessarily opposed to plurality, novelty, or creativity. I believe that not only are persons distinctive in that the unity of one's life history is self-imposed, but also that unity is a need for persons. This does not entail that everyone actually strives for it, any more than the fact that health is a need entails that everyone actually strives for that. We need unity in order to understand our own thoughts and actions. Self-knowledge requires it. Our self-knowledge is not an aggregate of information. It is a conception of our individuality that is faithful to what it comprises. Whatever we undertake, unified self-understanding promotes its success. We undeniably have a teleological nature, if only in the minimal sense that we select and pursue ends. To unify one's life history is not to confine that teleology to a single end or to limit oneself. It is to see how and why one goes about what one does. It illuminates and informs the exercises of one's capacities. It is a manner of self-definition.

The rational regulation of capacities for self-determination facilitates unity. Rational regulation here is not the sort of formalism Kant is often accused of. Moreover, in striving to realize the natural teleology of the self one does not typically think in terms of such abstract notions as self-enjoy-

---

[15]B. Williams, *Morality, An Introduction to Ethics*, Harper & Row, New York, 1972, p. 64.

ment and rational self-determination. Our judgments and deliberations usually concern contingencies of our circumstances and our feelings and relations with others, and so forth. But these figure in our life histories and are related to our happiness and conceptions of ourselves because they are the "matter" so to speak informed by the teleology of self-enjoyment and self-determination. Our impulses, needs, and desires always figure in our motivations. The issue is the *manner* in which they figure. A person can have intensely strong passions *and* self-mastery. The latter does not cancel or deny the former. It organizes and moderates them as they are translated into motive and act. And I have argued that virtue is a mode of successful rational regulation. It is a distortion to regard virtue as an enemy of appetite and affect, or as a suppression of one's individuality or authenticity.

These latter are not simple notions of spontaneous expression, as though they were promoted by absense of restraint. They involve expression. But they also involve self-knowledge and a kind of self-possession. These are the crucial elements in integrating personality, and they are not possible without a responsible effort at interpretation of one's character, tendencies, and drives. Self-determination is unguided without this sort of integrity and conscious, reflective self-appreciation. Rational self-mastery and virtue do not make us all alike. They do not level individuality. They impart to it the measure of construction on our own part that makes it valuable, and a constituent of self-enjoyment. They do this through their contribution to intelligible unity. Self-determination realizes value for us in so far as we understand its operation. It is not the pleasure that our actions cause which is of primary importance, but that our agency is directed through our own authority. As I argued earlier, self-enjoyment is achieved through striving to realize a constellation of specific ends, and these and their relations and weights may be altered. How one interprets the unity of his or her life history can be a factor in how these are altered. But unity is the key to the intelligibility of one's life history. As such, it is crucial to effective exercise of capacities for self-determination.

The critique of rational self-mastery was as much a critique of the idea of unity as of the idea of freedom's having an intrinsic end. The two jointly constitute the teleology of personhood. It was this metaphysic which was rejected. But in rejecting it we throw out too much. The nature of persons is plastic, but it is not a material which one can fashion into just anything or which has no limiting contours. To eviscerate it of teleology is to dissolve it in a manner that does not allow of reconstitution. The recognition of these limits is not an act of voluntary confinement. Rather, these limits provide a framework for self-understanding and the understanding of others.

Candidates for the first principles of practical reason have always been offered by philosophers, from Plato's principle of psychic harmony, to Mill's principle of Utility. All have had defects, emphasizing certain values over others, preferring certain ends to others. But they are attempts at a normative understanding of personal nature. These principles of rationality can be abusively or repressively employed. Plato and Aristotle reserved virtue and happiness for the cultured and leisured. Kant demanded formal satisfiability at the expense of complex and variable human needs and circumstances. And so on and on. The literary and philosophical critics of the rationally regulated teleology of persons have done much to expose defects in the presentations of it and to add to our understanding of the complexity of its phenomenology and dynamics. But, as a general explanatory conception the rational teleology view remains the most satisfactory unifying account of the phenomena. Central among these are the issues of freedom, unity, rationality, and moral value, and how they interdependently figure in the course and understanding of a personal life history.

Conclusion

Relativism, Tradition, and Objectivity

I have tried to delineate the main contours of a theory of personal nature and how it grounds conceptions of moral value and moral motivation. In the previous chapter I defended the account against some criticisms and alternatives. Here I address the issue of relativism and its bearing on the account of persons and morality. There are many different types of and approaches to relativism. Even a general survey of the subject from Protagoras to the present would be too complicated and ambitious for my purposes here. I will confine myself to one general type of relativism. This I shall call the "tradition-bound" approach to relativism. There are two reasons for discussing it. First, the topic of tradition has justifiably received a good deal of attention in recent years. Second, my own account may appear to be a variant of one or more influential traditions, though I have claimed that moral theorizing can be objective in a way that relativism does not accommodate. So, I shall try to describe this sort of relativism and defend my own claims against it.

I will not enter into the discussion of how best to understand or analyze the concept of tradition. I expect a serviceable and familiar understanding of it exists. But it is so important because if moral beliefs and practices must be understood as relativized to traditions and their contexts and conventions, then there is no objective standpoint from which conceptions of what persons are, what the nature of moral value is, and what the criteria and application of moral judgment are can be assessed and validated.

A theory of persons and moral psychology with no regard for the importance of context and tradition would be seriously flawed. But this is not reason enough to make theorizing about the nature of persons, moral psychology, and ethics essentially tradition-bound. We must be careful not to become reductionist in our tendency to explain phenomena in terms of it. A focus of attention in explaining what it is to be a person and what virtue is that is not expressed by the tradition-bound is needed. MacIntyre, in his discussion, says, "A living tradition then is an historically extended, socially embodied argument, and an argument precisely in part about the goods which constitute that tradition."[1] And he says, "Moreover when a tradition is in good order it is always partially constituted by an argument about the goods the pursuit of which gives to that tradition its particular point and purpose."[2]

It is important to notice that in chapter 15 of *After Virtue* MacIntyre is talking about tradition in a certain restricted sense and he is careful to spell out what he means by a *living* tradition. Tradition, both in his restricted sense and in the broader sense of what is done customarily, what is handed down, institutionalized and so forth is of course present in just about every aspect of our lives and its influence is powerful. It is sometimes so powerful that we want to strive to break free of it, or recast the "argument." Elements from tradition, elements that define and clarify our context, vocabulary, and patterns of explanation and justification are unavoidable and need to be acknowledged in fashioning our concepts of persons and virtue. But while tradition is unavoidable in this way we should not exaggerate its justificatory significance. That would run the risk of assimilating being morally good into being good at what the tradition commends or encourages. The virtues are habits which are excellences, but they are not just a matter of being excellent at certain socially sanctioned habits.

Moreover, traditions supply a ready and well-stocked inventory of vocabulary, criteria, and precedents that can be critically or uncritically appropriated to provide rationalizations. They can, in this manner, offer too much, and one may selectively avail oneself of the offering. This will include not only variants within a tradition, but hybrids, confusions, and aggregates or fragments of traditions that include not only some widely held moral beliefs and practices, but also borrowings from social and occupational roles and even family traditions. For example, when one enters a profession he may encounter many traditions and many *kinds* of

---

[1]A. MacIntyre, *After Virtue*, University of Notre Dame Press, Notre Dame, IN, 1981, p. 207.

[2]Ibid, p. 206.

traditions. Consider medicine. There are numerous traditions associated with the healing arts and their purposes and role in the culture. There may also be traditions of state organization, licensing, and control, for example. The members may see themselves as agents of state institutions because of this, as many German physicians apparently did in the years prior to and during the Second World War. There are also often traditions of social standing for the members of the profession, and they may have a good deal of authority over not just lower-ranked members of their profession and other personnel but also their patients. In some communities the technical expertise or professional standing of some groups are regarded as marks of the possession of good judgement over all variety of matters. Within a profession there will certainly be traditions concerning standards of competence and propriety and perhaps even what one can "get away" with. Social, economic, family, scientific, and other factors, each not only with histories, but with their own traditions, can and do come into play in complex, variable interactions. These are not just patterns of behavior. They also involve relations of authority, standards of evaluation, and the inculcation of certain attitudes toward oneself and toward members of other groups and outsiders. Evidence of such phenomena is easy to observe in medicine, business, the military, government, academia, and labor unions to mention only a few examples. The traditions differ in different societies, but there are such traditions in each.

While practices and even styles of reasoning will fit more or less into certain traditional patterns, there is no assurance that the tradition is in general morally sound or that the participants will not go in for a sort of complacency, where the justification of a practice is "this is what we do." What MacIntyre calls the argument must be kept alive and its logic must not degenerate. Appealing to the authority of tradition is not unjustified in itself. It is a question of the justification of the tradition.

Practices are shaped by and shape contexts. But it just does not follow from this that the general and basic character of morality is determined by practice, or that the nature of persons and the virtues are cultural products. Consider examples concerning courage. When we observe that until fairly recently people had to have amputations performed, give birth and so on without pain killers, sophisticated equipment and procedures and anesthetic it might seem that they were somehow less sensitive to certain types of pain. But they weren't. They were less fearful of them. They were more accustomed to seeing animals (and their fellows) maimed and killed than we are. There were types of pain and fear that they had to manage better than we do. This is not to say we are somehow *more* fearful people. We manage other types of fear, the fears and pains that our circumstances typically involve. Courage is not a different characteristic than it used to be. But the ways in which many people need to be courageous have changed and even differ within societies at a time. Or, in a wine-drinking society temperance may seem a different thing than in a teetotalling society. But it is the expression or practice of it that varies in some ways, not the characteristic, just as charitable practices and their attendant rituals differ. But we can still judge whether the practices are serving the good of the practitioners and are rational. We can evaluate the content of the tradition or conventions as well as how well people conform to them. This is not just a matter of *contrasting* them with our own traditions but still refusing or being unable to judge them objectively. We can so judge them.

One could argue that the account presented here is a variant of themes in a long-standing Western tradition of philosophical theorizing, but that there is no "pure" impersonal standpoint from which to theorize that is not shaped along certain cultural-historical lines. The best one can do is articulate a tradition or initiate changes in it, perhaps radical changes. But we cannot fully step back from or out of our position in an essentially historical human world. Still, that the human world is historical is not to say that our understanding of it must be historicist, or relativist, or merely ideological. Facts, especially normative facts, are never self-presenting. We have to adopt commitments, pursue certain avenues of inquiry, respond to felt needs and available inducements. But there is a kind of accessible bestness apart from strength of preference or power of tradition. I think that in the practical realm, analogously to the theoretical realm, we must strive to approximate to an ideal that we do not have altogether clearly in sight at the outset. That is, we have an image of explanatoriness, objectivity, rationality, and so on which is not fixed for us beforehand, but which is elaborated and calibrated as we go on. The ideal comes closer into view piece by piece and does not emerge as a whole. At one time linguistic, at another psychological, at another anthropological and at another time logical issues receive heightened attention. Insights that penetrate and methods that explain do not come according to any schedule fixed in advance.

But I believe that in striving for this ideal we need to keep before us an objective focus of attention. By this I mean we need to strive to develop an understanding of our nature and moral reasoning and not choose the option of pretending that our understanding of these cannot be improved and appraised with reference to real constraints. We do not make our nature and we do not invent basic needs and goods and how best to fulfill and achieve them. The view that our values, moral perspectives, and what it is to live well are ungrounded or are fictions or have nothing to do with objective considerations is unsustainable. We live in a world we did not create and we are constrained by that world, what we are, and our understanding of those things. What is needed is greater understanding, not a terror of or contempt for objectivity. I believe that striving for an objective understanding in ethics is part of taking other people morally seriously, regarding them as equally real persons. Regarding them as equally real as oneself is not just a matter of seeing them as enough like oneself to accord them equal status, as though they were honorary members of a club or morally housebroken. It is instead a matter of enriching an understanding of what it is to be a person that is not prefigured by local or contextual circumstances and contingent needs and goals.

It is part of the conception of personal nature that virtue is a constituent of successfully realizing the potentialities of that nature. We are constituted of certain capacities and an understanding of them involves appreciation of a notion of their well-ordering. While it doesn't in itself entail motivational commitments, it does orient and rationalize them. It provides an objective focus of attention. It is my belief that this understanding, while it is articulated in a context of certain traditions, is not bound or confined by them.

The relativist is right that claims of objectivity and rationality have not lived up to their pretensions and have been used to license all variety of awful beliefs and practices. People don't like to think of their attitudes and practices as lacking justification. We fill the lack with rationalizations and use these as a cloak for force, fraud, and self-deception. But the way out of this history of errors is not to transform morality by freeing it from the constraints of logic and understanding. Nietzsche, who found so much to object to in traditions masquerading as objectivity, wrote:

> Indeed, we philosophers and "free spirits" feel as if a new dawn were shining on us when we receive the tidings the "the old god is dead"; our heart overflows with gratitude, amazement, anticipation, expectation. At last the horizon appears free again to us, even granted that it is not bright; at last our ships may venture out again, venture out to face any danger; all the daring of the lover of knowledge is permitted again; the sea, our sea, lies open again; perhaps there has never yet been such an "open sea."[3]

But neither is his sort of rebellion against rationality not the way out. Unless one is antecedently committed to some sorts of recognizable values that are susceptible to criticism and appraisal with respect to objective considerations it is hard to see how this is liberating, or indeed what repression or liberation is supposed to be. How are we to identify, formulate, and address moral issues if the material from which our interpretations are constructed does not have properties of its own that limit what can be done with it?

Part of the appeal of relativism lies in its faulty caricature of what it opposes. If the relativist claims that objectivity and rationality require fixed, a priori, or self-evident conditions then he has made a mistake. Objectivity and rationality are conceptions we aim at, not that we begin with, and they must be elaborated and not simply discovered. But their significance con-

[3]From "Fearlessness," in *The Gay Science, The Portable Nietzsche,* ed. and tr. W. Kaufmann, Viking Press, New York, NY, 1954, pp. 447–448.

sists in the authority they impart to judgments and claims. This is the authority of shared acknowledgements (or at least the real, and non-accidental possibility of them). Perhaps the authoritativeness of the conceptions is not up to the standards of some sort of absolutism, involving fixity, necessity, or some sort of cognitive transparency. But they need not involve that absolutism to be authoritative in the sense of expressing shared acknowledgements that reflect criteria of judgment sufficient to distinguish error from correctness. The relativist may say that his view accommodates this, but it does not really. If relativism is true then moral disagreements are not to be adjudicated by application of such criteria. I am appealing to a non-relativist notion of judgmental or rational efficacy. I believe we can and must.

This is not to say that the relativist does not or cannot take moral matters very seriously. It is a question of how moral thinking is to be directed. According to relativism, there are limiting conditions on the reach of moral thinking and justification. This is not a diminution of the reality or significance of moral matters. But it is a constraint on what is accessible for the interpretation and resolution of moral disagreements and for informing moral judgment. My objection to both relativism in general and the tradition-bound approach in particular is not just that they extend too liberal a license for moral beliefs and practices, or that they may easily turn into a sort of complacency, in the sense of justification by sheer weight of tradition and convention. I think these *are* defects of these views, but not the central one. The central defect is that they both dispense with the notion of objective rationality. It is not just what they may let in that is objectionable, but what they keep out. What they keep out is that there is a best way to understand moral phenomena. It is one thing to allow for diversity in moral views and to allow for groups and even individuals to choose and adopt their own moral beliefs and practices. And it is necessary to acknowledge the context-dependencies these involve. But none of this refutes or renders incoherent the notion that as far as the explanatory and justificatory situations are concerned, there are better and worse descriptions, understandings, and presentations and that these can be very significant for practice. That there are such qualitative distinctions between insights and theories leaves room for objective rationality, for an account that admits of revision and correction by means other than fiat, decision, simple preference, or various brands of non-rational causality and influence.

There is an oft exaggerated tendency to contrast the conventional in morality with the rational, as if they excluded each other and there were no traffic between them. Of course morality is conventional in the sense that its practices and standards are exhibited in shared and variable and revisable social and institutional arrangements. As James Wallace observed, "In studying human life, then, one is studying something that is naturally, characteristically, and distinctively conventional."[4] But conventions can be well or badly rationalized and more or less reflect objective considerations. The conventions of morality are not rationally unaccountable.[5] If we take relativism seriously, then shared conceptions of moral issues and terms of engagement with others in argument and appraisal or even the possibility of them, will have a very tenuous status. Agreement, or the possibility of it, will not even potentially have a rational validation. This does not entail that different systems of beliefs and practices could not interpenetrate peacefully and that all traffic between them will end in destructive collision. But it does leave us without a perspective from which to recognize and appreciate the transactions. In striving for an objective understanding of moral phenomena we appreciate them as phenomena in one world no portions of which are more or less real than others. This makes it possible for us to unify the diversity of moral perspectives, concerns, and practices. Rationality is what gives us access to different moralities and makes possible criticism of one's own.

A proper understanding of morality involves appreciating how our conceptions and practices constitute a second nature for us, which is a realization (for better or worse) of our primary nature. If there is genuine, objective practical wisdom it is knowledge of that primary nature and its relation to a morally well-ordered second nature. Relativism has no room for practical wisdom, only room for conventional wisdom. As such it eliminates a crucial condition for a correct regard for other people as morally

[4]J. D. Wallace, *Virtues and Vices*, Cornell University Press, Ithaca, NY, 1978, p. 34

[5]A further area of difficulty we should acknowledge has to do with drawing the line or lines between manners and morals. It is extremely difficult to do this since some matters of etiquette are not mere formalities and may have moral significance, and also our moral beliefs and practices are manifested in customs and conventions of explanation and action. if I am waiting impatiently in line at a movie theatre and shove the man in front of me I am not only being rude but also acting in a way that can needlessly harm others. If I am content to mutter obscenities under my breath, that may seem less of a morally relevant act, even if I offend and horrify others with the zeal and creativity of my profanity. But there are places where offense turns into harm, as with spray painting synagogues with swastikas or in racial intimidation in the ritualistic manner of the Ku Klux Klan. This is a kind of emotional terrorism and is meant to express malice, unlike the foul-mouthed movie goer who confines himself to expressing annoyance.

Also, it is often even more difficult to make clear distinctions between manners and morals when confronted with unfamiliar and very different societies. One feels awkward and ill at ease about gestures, appropriate responses and so forth. One's simple ignorance can easily be interpreted as insensitivity or arrogance.

But the deepest problem in these matters is not that morality just is social or cultural convention or that moral conceptions are incommensurable or not rationally accessible. Before even raising those issues people have to deal with the more basic problem of ignorance of beliefs, justifications, and practices of others. Mere difference is no premise for relativism unless the differences must be understood relativistically. But first we need to have a detailed, nuanced understanding of what we and others are about. The increase in understanding will broaden the context in which terms of acknowledgement, justification, and argument can be effective.

real. It leaves the open question of who is to count as a person and in what manner and what is the scope of moral concepts and commitments. On relativistic grounds the inclusion of others as equal inhabitants of the moral world is optional. Moral personality is thus conferred upon others according to how they *fit* into our (whoever *we* are) scheme of conceptions, evaluations and practices. If, according to one system, some group is so despised as to be regarded as less than fully morally real the relativist can object but has disallowed himself any resources to show this a mistake, a genuine wrong and not just something repellent.

We must distinguish between the conventions and conceptions through which a group appreciates what it is to be a person and an objective account of our nature. Even an articulate, long-standing version of the former may be badly wrongheaded. We should not confuse the seemingly unlimited possibilities of what we can do, with a totally elastic conception of what we can be. One potential danger of tradition-bound relativism is that we know that we can think of others and even think of ourselves in morally inappropriate and inaccurate terms. For example, Roger Taney, former Chief Justice of the United States Supreme Court, argued in his decision of the Dred Scott case in 1857 that slaves were not citizens and could not sue in Federal Court. A suit had been brought on behalf of Scott who was a slave who had been to free territory and was then returned to slavery. The suit was brought to return him to freedom. But slaves and even free descendants of slaves were not recognized as possessing the rights and privileges that belonged to whites. Justice Taney was not explicitly arguing on relativistic grounds. But they were relativistic in a tradition-bound way. Tradition-bound relativism involves a discontinuity between one's own morality and the moralities of others. This is a kind of disengagement, a way of putting the morality of others at a distance as though territorial limits could be drawn.

In the Introduction I noted that even if there were objective moral considerations it would not follow that people would guide their actions by them, and I suspect that this fact is sometimes used to make room for relativism. Gilbert Harman in "Relativistic Ethics: Morality as Politics" remarks that:

> You cannot always argue someone into being moral. Much depends on his or her antecedent interests and principles. If his or her principles and interests diverge sufficiently from yours, it may well happen that he or she has no reason to accept your morality.[6]

He is right that you can't always argue people into being moral. But what is asserted in the third sentence of the quote doesn't follow from that, nor do I believe it to be true on its own. Even if there are widely acknowl-

---

[6]G. Harman, "Relativistic Ethics: Morality as Politics", in *Midwest Studies in Philosophy*, Vol. III, University of Minnesota Press, Minneapolis, MN, 1980, p. 110.

edged and understood objective considerations that shape moral judgment and evaluation, this alone would not make people good. What reasons there are to be moral do not entail how people will act. The actual facts of how and why people act do not reflect the best reasons for action, and there is no logic which can bridge the gap. But it would be a mistake, and one that is frequently committed, to regard this situation as indicating the impossibility of objectivity in ethics in the sense of reasons that apply to anyone, as though lack of acceptance implied lack of truth. We know that sound arguments are not necessarily convincing and that even unsound ones are often accepted. This is not a failure of logical theory but a failure of logical behavior. It is no reason to dispense with logic. Similarly, a failure of moral reasons or moral understanding to be translated into practice does not discredit the theory. We can't, for example, *make* relativism true by acting irrationally or vilifying objectivity.

I have not attempted to explain how the account of the moral phenomena I have presented is related to moral education. I am not making my conclusion the dismal acknowledgement that objectivity and rationality can get no purchase on motivation. They can. But the logic of conviction and commitment is not identical to the logic of explanation. The latter, through the aid of philosophy, can do a great deal to show us the way. It is not a matter of philosophical adjudication whether we go that way.

Index